BEFORE YOU QUIT TEACHING

Tools, Resources, and Hope for New Teachers in High-Poverty Classrooms

Ruby K. Payne
Before You Quit Teaching:
Tools, Resources, and Hope for
New Teachers in High-Poverty Classrooms

136 pages; Bibliography pages 132–133

ISBN: 978-1-948244-25-1

© 2019 by aha! Process, Inc.
All rights reserved. No part of this book may be reproduced in any manner whatsoever without written permission, except in the case of brief quotations embedded in critical articles and reviews.

For information, contact:
aha! Process, Inc., P.O. Box 727, Highlands, TX 77562-0727;
(800) 424-9484 ▪ (281) 426-5300; www.ahaprocess.com

Instagram, Facebook, PDF, and other versions available free online:
ahaprocess.com/byqt

BEFORE YOU QUIT TEACHING

Tools, Resources, and Hope for New Teachers in High-Poverty Classrooms

RUBY K. PAYNE, PH.D.

Section I Hope 2

- **1** Introduction: If I can do it, you can do it 3
- **2** Purpose of the book 14
- **3** Hope and skills 18
- **4** Your hope for your own life 20
- **5** The bigger picture of your life 24

Section II Self-Assessment and My Future Story 26

- **6** Basic adult development tasks 27
- **7** How does adult development impact the classroom and campus? 36
- **8** Value proposition 42
- **9** Future story 46
- **10** Self-assessment 50

Section III Tools and Resources for Daily Stressors 54

- **11** The daily stressors and frustrations: How to deal with them 55
- **12** Tools to de-stress 62
- **13** Resources, solutions, and insights to help you stay in teaching if you are in a high-poverty school ... 70
- **14** Students 72
- **15** Discipline and classroom management 82

This book was originally created as a digital product; full resources/videos available at *ahaprocess.com/byqt*

Section IV Parents, Principals, Peers 90

16 Parents: Why don't they come to events like parent-teacher conferences? Don't they care?..... 91

17 Will the principal support me? 96

18 What do you do when you have a difficult principal? What is a difficult principal? 102

19 Colleagues—will they help me or hinder me?..... 108

20 Curriculum and instruction—
I only have so much time 112

Section V Realities of Teaching 116

21 Issues at the middle and secondary levels 117

22 Working conditions 119

23 Politics, morale, and unions 120

24 Emotional realities of teaching:
How to handle the grieving 122

25 Conclusion 125

Section VI Bonus 126

Expert Secondary Principal Rubric 127

Expert Elementary Principal Rubric 130

Selected Bibliography 132

Before You Quit Teaching • **Table of Contents**

Full resources/videos available at *ahaprocess.com/byqt*

1 Introduction: If I Can Do It, You Can Do It

tldr: The first two years are difficult for everyone. Even colleagues can be a challenge. With mentorship, there is room for growth and advancement in the education profession.

The first two years of teaching are simply SURVIVAL. My own experience was no different than many others'.

I had always wanted to teach. I never played with dolls the way you were supposed to, by making a little family and playing house. Instead, I would line them up in neat rows and teach them lessons in English and history.

My student teaching experience in a middle school was brutal. It was so stressful that I would throw up many mornings before I went to the school. My supervising teacher was callous and uncaring toward me, toward the students, and, as I later learned, toward her own children.

Ruby Payne
Introduction to *Before You Quit Teaching*

The way the program was supposed to work was that you were to student teach for six weeks. The first week you were supposed to do one class, the second week two classes, etc., until you were teaching a full day. That is not the way mine went.

The first week I was there, the supervising teacher said, "Okay, starting next week you will teach all day, all six classes. This is a break for me. And, by the way, I am way behind on grading," and she gave me a stack of papers to grade that was two feet high. Last, but not least, she told me that I would occasionally need to babysit her children on the weekends! I was waiting tables at the time and could make up to $100 in tips on a good night. For a three- to four-hour evening of babysitting, the supervising teacher would give me $1. But I babysat because I really wanted to teach, and I wanted a good recommendation.

Full resources/videos available at *ahaprocess.com/byqt*

Organization of the Book

I
Hope

II
Self-Assessment and My Future Story

III
Tools and Resources for Daily Stressors

IV
Parents, Principals, Peers

V
Realities of Teaching

VI
Bonus

After I graduated, my first teaching job was in a high school in a rural area of northern Indiana. When you are a beginning teacher at the high school, you get freshmen. I taught five classes of freshman English. For whatever reason, a disproportionate amount of my students were boys.

I was also doing the drama productions—one each semester. For a couple months each semester, I was up at the school for three extra hours a night practicing and rehearsing the play.

The English department was a disaster. There were six people, all of us very different personalities.

Kate was really a French teacher who wanted to teach French but had settled for English. Nevertheless, she was a very good teacher. She was seasoned, had lived in France, loved basketball, was divorced, and loved French wine.

Leonard, a beginning teacher, was quiet, a bit afraid of his own shadow, hesitant to voice an opinion, and very diplomatic in anything he did say.

Joyce really liked to sit in a chair, was a bully, had two children, and talked about how the students were "empty buckets" and we had to "fill them up."

Jean was a musician, a singer, and believed in a very academic approach to literature. She told me that no one could live without knowing Shakespeare. I said, "I reckon people DO live without knowing Shakespeare," whereupon Jean burst into tears.

Andrew was the fifth teacher. He was an arrogant pseudointellectual—everything was beneath him. He considered himself an aspiring writer as yet undiscovered. A renaissance man without the charm or experience. The rest of us peons in the department were to be merely tolerated, if not outright disliked.

And then there was me. Unafraid to voice an opinion, I enjoyed students—especially the outliers in the room: the badly behaved, the gifted, the unusual, the shy.

I was unintimidated by the disruptive boys (I had three brothers) and the disrespectful girls. And truly, I was not a very good teacher when I started. I am surprised that they did not fire me!

Something I was good at was producing the school plays— good enough to cause some jealousy in the department, anyway. One year, Joyce turned me in to the legal department of the company that printed the scripts for the theater productions because she said I had violated copyright laws. Joyce had been doing the theater productions prior to me but did not want to keep doing them. However, after I took over, Joyce did not like the success I was having. Yes, professional jealousy is real, and it can contribute to a negative work environment. In my second year, the school was vandalized. They broke the windows in the English office. When the police came, they said, "Look what they did to that desk," and pointed to Joyce's desk. With little charity in my voice, I told them that her desk always looked that way.

The principal my first year was ineffective. He actually took my classroom away from me midyear because a teacher (whose family owned the bank) had decided that she needed two classrooms in which to teach—mine and hers. The principal gave her mine and put me in the bleachers in the gym. After a week of this,

I went to him and told him that if he did not give my room back to me, I would go to the school board meeting. I told him I thought they would not look kindly on one teacher having two classrooms and me having none. I got my room back. My second year, we had a new principal who was terrified of the students. He would lock himself in his office, come out at lunch and get the mail, and then lock himself back in his office until the end of the day.

The students were in a rural area where education was not highly valued. People there went to school because it was required. Among the many students I had, there were a couple students who came to class drunk, one who was working for the pharmacy and helping herself to the pills, one who crawled under the desks to look up girls' skirts, and one who had a nearly perfect memory. He remembered everything I ever said and could quote it back exactly as I had said it. My point is that not every student had negative behavioral issues. However, I had one class that was so behaviorally difficult that I was never sure how I would keep them in line for that 45 minutes every day. Some classes are such a mix of very difficult personalities that it can feel like there are no strategies that will work.

Ruby Payne Origin Story

But I was lucky. I had an unexpected mentor—the assistant principal at the time taught me to teach. He asked all of us who taught a particular course to give the same assignment and bring the student papers to a meeting. Then he asked us to pick a low-, middle-, and high-scoring paper and lay them on the table. Kate's lowest-scoring student paper was a better performance than my highest-scoring student paper. (As I said, I was not a very good teacher.)

> **I learned that student performance is the most important indicator of how well you teach.**

The first thing out of my mouth was, "Kate, you have better students than I do."

She said to me, "I have Roger. You want him?"

Well, I knew Roger, and I did not want him. And then I thought about her students and realized that she actually did not have better students than I did. I did not say another word in that meeting, but afterward, I went to her and said, "Tell me how you got that performance." And she did.

I learned that student performance is the most important indicator of how well you teach. It is not the teacher evaluation instrument, but what you can actually get students to do. I knew that was true in theater and performing arts generally, but I had never applied it at that level in teaching. And then I did. The assistant principal's grading calibration exercise was a turning point for me, and his guidance continued to be valuable through my time as a classroom teacher and later in my career.

Research shows that if you do not have a professional mentor in your 20s, it is a developmental handicap for your career.

So find a mentor.

During my third and fourth years of teaching, I went back to school and got a master's degree in English. I drove an hour and a half to Western Michigan University twice a week for two years. Why? At that time in Indiana, if you did not have a master's degree after five years of teaching, you could not get your teaching certificate renewed.

I continued teaching at the school in Indiana for six years. At the end of that time, between theater productions and graduate school, I was burned out. The administrative politics, the constant demands, and the students I could not help all took a toll on me, so I took a year off from teaching, I explored other options, and I realized that teaching was where I belonged.

When I came back, my teaching opportunities expanded. I became a department chair, then I went to the central office to work on curriculum and instruction, and then to two regional service centers—one in Texas and one in Illinois—then I went on to be an elementary principal. From there I became director of professional development, and then I wrote a book that took me to a national consulting level. Many individuals think that the career path in education is limited. It is not. **There are multiple opportunities to lead and teach.**

2 Purpose of the Book

tldr: The purpose of the book is to tell you things I wish I'd known when I started teaching. Why should you listen to me? I care about you as much as I care about students. Why is teaching so hard? Schools can't keep up with changes. Will teaching ever be worth it? Yes, and here's how to get there…

The purpose of this book is to help you have an easier transition from college into teaching than I did. I wish someone had explained to me some of the things I will explain to you and had given me some tools and resources.

If you are a beginning teacher, the school probably gave you the students with the least amount of financial resources and some of the most difficult emotional issues. If you are like most beginning teachers, after the first six weeks of school, you are SERIOUSLY thinking about quitting.

Before you quit, I want to share with you some hope, resources, and a future story.

First and foremost, this book is about you.

I want you to be happy and fulfilled as a teacher. But in order to be fulfilled, you need to answer some questions for yourself. After we go over those questions, if you do decide to stay in teaching, then I have outlined resources that will help make it fulfilling and meaningful for you.

Why would you pay attention to my advice? For the last 23 years, I have spent my time speaking to more than 1 million educators about students from poverty. I have listened to their stories. In the last year I helped a school district get off of "improvement required" status in one year. Before that, I taught at the high school level for nine years, and I have been an elementary principal. I spent six years in two different regional service centers helping school districts and campuses raise their test scores. But most of all, you should listen to my advice because I care about teachers as much as I care about students.

You have chosen one of the hardest jobs to do, but it does get better, and there is room to grow.

> Before you quit, I want to share with you some hope, resources, and a future story.

Why Is Teaching So Difficult Now?

1. A higher percentage of children are in poverty or near poverty than in the past

2. There is a greater level of instability for children in poverty because of mobility, changing relationships, cost of housing, etc.

3. A higher number of children have behavioral and emotional issues (anxiety, anger, avoidance, etc.)

4. State curriculum and assessment has become more rigorous and difficult

5. Teachers receive less support from parents now than they did in the past

6. Many schools have inadequate facilities and equipment

7. Political changes and instability in the administration

8. Administrative systems have become more complex in ways that do not necessarily benefit students

"Don't worry, the expectations are the same as ever ... only completely different."

How do you develop hope, resources, and a future story for yourself and your students?

Full resources/videos available at ahaprocess.com/byqt

Why do school districts give the most challenging students to beginning teachers? Teachers with experience can use assets like seniority, tenure, and union work agreements to bid out of those jobs and work in schools with more resourced student populations. This is just one of many reasons teacher turnover rates are so high in the first two years.

So if basically everything about the job is a challenge, why would you even consider staying? Because it will make your life much more meaningful.

In the research, if you have a mission or a cause, life is much more meaningful. As a friend of mine said to me, "Ruby, when I was teaching, I felt like I was making a difference. When we moved and I had to take whatever job was available and wound up selling business technology, I didn't feel that way. **These children need YOU more than ever before.** For many of your students, you will open a new world to them—one of possibility and hope." When she said that to me, she gave me possibility and hope for this book.

3 Hope and Skills

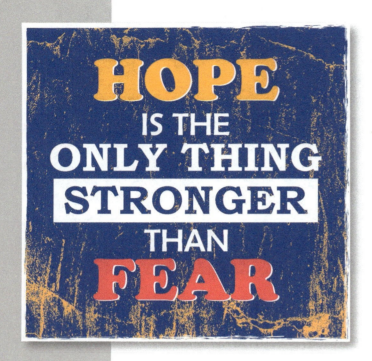

tldr: The teachers you had growing up can inspire hope. Not all of them, but focus on the positive! Your best teachers probably had most of the skills listed below. Build those skills in yourself.

Identify three teachers who made a difference for you. How did they impact your life?

1.

2.

3.

Why do you want to be a teacher?

What hope do you want to bring to your students?

My inspiration for being a teacher was Mrs. Morgan, my second-grade teacher. I loved her. I decided I would be like her—I loved how she looked and smiled. And she was a fabulous teacher. Very fair.

Most Teachers Do Not Get into Teaching for the Money. They Want to Make a Difference.

In the research, these are the characteristics of teachers who were effective; i.e., "these teachers made the most significant impact" on the lives of their students.

Here's what students said over a 15-year period of data collection.

The teacher:

- ❏ Came to class prepared
- ❏ Maintained positive attitudes about teaching and about students
- ❏ Held high expectations for all students
- ❏ Showed creativity in teaching the class
- ❏ Treated and graded students fairly
- ❏ Displayed a personal, approachable touch with students
- ❏ Cultivated a sense of belonging in the classroom
- ❏ Dealt with student problems compassionately
- ❏ Had a sense of humor and did not take everything seriously
- ❏ Respected students and did not deliberately embarrass them
- ❏ Was forgiving and did not hold grudges
- ❏ Admitted mistakes

Your ability to bring these skills to your students has to do with how much you know about yourself.

4 Your Hope for Your Own Life

tldr: Adults have stages of development, and people in their 20s develop a worldview, enter the world of work, have romantic relationships, and form their concept of what adults "should" do. Accept teaching as one piece of the larger picture of your life, not the whole thing. Don't get caught up in the day-to-day.

If you are going to keep your work-life balance, it becomes especially important that you know a little about the developmental stages adults go through. Just like teenagers have developmental stages, so do adults, and these are well-documented.

When you are in your 20s, you have these developmental tasks: identity (who you are), intimacy (who you are in relationship to another), and independence (what you are able to do on your own). During this decade, you have to develop a worldview, figure out some sort of work experience, have some sort of relationship experience(s), and figure out what an adult "should" do. The research is that if you marry in your 20s, you often marry someone who is a replacement for one of your parents. The only thing that you are sure of in your 20s is that you DO NOT want to be like your parents.

As I mentioned earlier, if you do not have a mentor in your professional life in your 20s, this can be a developmental handicap for the rest of your work life.

Between the approximate ages of 28 and 32, adults reevaluate every decision they made in their 20s. A Johns Hopkins University study indicated that adult personality is not formed until you are around 29. In that time window of 28–32 (approximately—some do it earlier, some later), relationships, work, career, etc. are all reexamined. For the last 50 years, first divorces for men occur at 30, and first divorces occur for women at 28. It is also in this timeframe that the biological clock starts ticking for women in terms of having a child. In the U.S., a woman with a B.S. or B.A. degree typically has her first child at 30 years of age.

One of the big things I recommend you think about in your 20s is the big picture of your life.

A book I would recommend to you is *The Defining Decade: Why Your Twenties Matter*. The psychologist who wrote this book, Meg Jay, is very clear that if you do not do the above developmental tasks in the decade of your 20s (develop a worldview, get work experience, have relationships, and decide what an adult "should" do), then you have lost 10 years of your lifetime and will experience real difficulty catching up.

One of the big things I recommend you think about in your 20s is the big picture of your life. This is something I did not consider when I was a beginning teacher in my 20s. It is very important to have work-life balance. In the research, family and friends are the top priorities in the lives of young people. Part of your satisfaction with teaching will be how you see teaching fitting into the larger frame of your life, as opposed to focusing on the day-to-day reality.

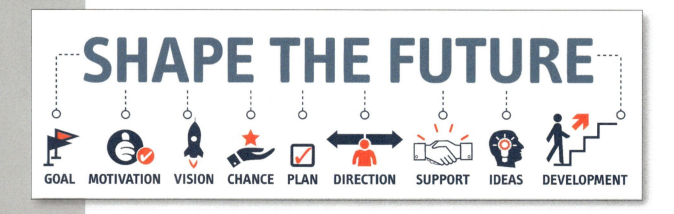

If you miss the forest for the trees, there may not be much to hold you in the job. When I came back to teaching after a year off, I could see teaching as a part of the larger frame of my life. This put it in a much better perspective for me than it had ever been in before.

The day-to-day aggravations of teaching became less able to spill over and affect the larger frame of my life.

5 The Bigger Picture of Your Life

tldr: Because the bigger picture of your life includes teaching, there is more room for other interests as well. Meditate on the bigger picture to find calm in stressful moments.

It is very important to have big-picture ideas for your life. Because you are a teacher and have two months off in the summer, you have more options than some other professionals do. When you start out, you may need to work during the summers to keep paying student loans on a beginning teacher's salary. But if you are not working to augment your salary, what can you pursue? Children? Travel? Money? Hobbies? Experiences? Career advancement? Graduate degrees? Relationships?

It is a deeply calming exercise to step back and look at the big picture.

Will all of this materialize? Not necessarily. But the extra time in the summer is a place to start focusing when you look at the big picture. People often say, "Someday I want to…" but then someday never comes. As a teacher, you'll have time to get a head start on someday.

Before you laugh about this, please remember that when your brain goes to a place of fear, worry, and discouragement, your blood flows to your brain stem and amygdala, AWAY from your cortex, which is where your thoughts are. If you have a big picture, you can go away from the fear and back to the thoughts and visualizations of your life in the bigger frame.

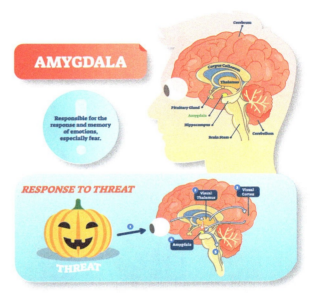

It is a deeply calming exercise to step back and look at the big picture.

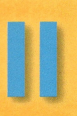

6 Basic Adult Development Tasks

tldr: With few exceptions, all adults experience distinct stages of development and are faced with tasks at each stage.

20s: Be an adult.

30s: Do I like adulting? How do I find balance?

40s: Coming to terms with own mortality brings more energy and purpose.

50s: 'No more BS.' What will I do with the time I have left?

60s and beyond: What is my legacy? How can I give back?

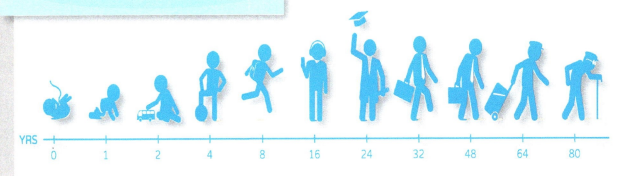

Basic Adult Development Tasks

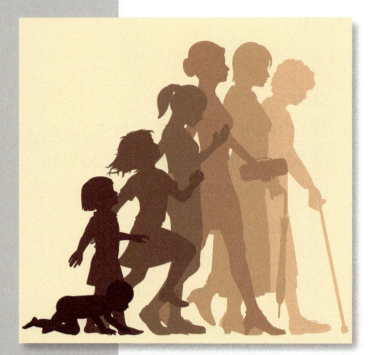

Regardless of race, country of origin, birth order, etc., these are developmental tasks that every adult faces.

Identity – Who am I?

Intimacy – Who am I in relationship to another?

Independence/autonomy – What can I do on my own?

Purpose/meaning – Why am I alive?

Work/role – What value do I bring?

Limitations of time – What do I do with the time I have?

Aging/death – How do I deal with the aging and death of others? How do I deal with my own aging and end-of-life issues?

All of these adult development tasks create emotional responses. Every individual has a choice to ignore or delay the development, but the issue will keep returning to be addressed.

AGE FRAME	TASKS/ISSUES/KEY QUESTIONS
18–22 'Pulling up roots'	**Key question: What am I going to do with my life?** **Four tasks:** Find a peer-group role, a sex role, an occupation, and a worldview/set of beliefs. Establish autonomy and identity. De-idealize the parent or parent substitute in order to start trusting own judgment. Big focus on what you do not want to do or be. In 2017, 30% of individuals under the age of 30 lived at home with their parents. These developmental tasks occur even if the individual is living at home. They may be delayed, but the issues of identity, intimacy, occupation, and a worldview/set of beliefs tend to develop.

Ruby Payne
Why Poverty Impacts Learning

AGE FRAME	TASKS/ISSUES/KEY QUESTIONS
22–28 *'Trying 20s'*	**Key question: What should I do to be an adult?** **Tasks:** Shape a dream, prepare for life's work, find a mentor, develop intimacy with another. Have a deep fear that choices are irrevocable. Strong belief that I will never be like my parents, that partners will grow together at equal speeds. A time of competing forces—stability and structure versus exploration and experimentation. Reasons for marriage in the 20s include: the need for safety, the need to fill some vacancy in yourself, the need to get away from home, the need for prestige or practicality. The presence or absence of a mentor at this time "has enormous impact on development … The lack of mentors … is a great developmental handicap." There is a tendency to marry someone who has many characteristics of or plays a similar role to one of our parents.

Full resources/videos available at *ahaprocess.com/byqt*

| AGE FRAME | TASKS/ISSUES/KEY QUESTIONS |

28–32

'Passage to the 30s'

Key question:
Do I agree with the adult that I am becoming?

Tasks: Revisit the decisions involving identity, intimacy, independence, marriage (lots of first divorces occur at this time), children (to have or not to have), career choices (do I really want to do this?), etc.

Strong belief that there is still time to do it all.

Women see it as a last chance in terms of children, career, and life path. Men often press the accelerator harder.

Marriage satisfaction decreases. "For the past 50 years, Americans have been most likely to break out of wedlock when the man is about 30 and the woman is about 28."

Learn that intelligence is not as well-rewarded as loyalty.

Learn that not all difficulties can be solved with willpower and intellect.

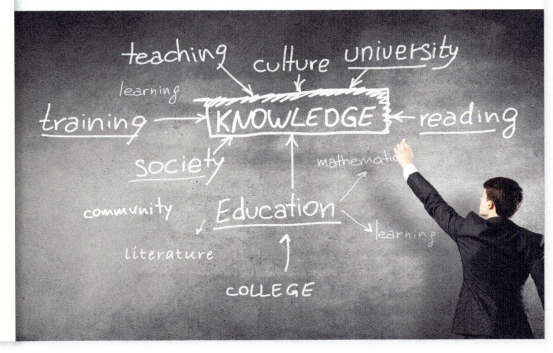

AGE FRAME	TASKS/ISSUES/KEY QUESTIONS
32–39 'Settling down'	**Key question: How do I achieve balance?** **Tasks:** "To sort out the qualities we want to retain from our childhood models, to blend them with the qualities and capacities that distinguish us as individuals, and to fit all this back together in some broader form." Women come "to understand that it is probably not possible for a woman to work out a combination of the two careers (domestic and extra-familial) until 30 or 35." Conflict between safety and autonomy, freedom and stability. Time is a huge issue—there is not enough. Squeezed between demands of children, career, aging parents, family dynamics. Strong defense of current beliefs. Fairly certain that their understanding/worldview is correct. 

| AGE FRAME | TASKS/ISSUES/KEY QUESTIONS |

35–45

'Authenticity crisis'

'Danger and opportunity'

'The adolescence of adulthood'

Key question:
Why am I doing this? What do I really believe?

Tasks: Aliveness versus stagnation. Shift in the sense of time—health, career, mortality (will not live forever). Changes happening in self and in others. New wrinkles appear every day. Taking apart the dream and its illusions to spark renewal.

Hormonal changes: Males start producing less testosterone, which allows estrogen to play more of a role (become more nurturing). Females produce less estrogen, and testosterone plays more of a role (become more assertive).

"The loss of youth, the faltering of physical powers we have always taken for granted, the fading purpose of stereotyped roles by which we have thus far identified ourselves, the spiritual dilemma of having no absolute answers—any or all of these shocks can throw us into crisis."

"Every loose end not resolved in previous passages will resurface to haunt us. These demons may lead us into private hells of depression, sexual promiscuity, power chasing, hypochondria, self-destructive acts (alcoholism, drug taking, car accidents, suicide), and violent swings of mood. All are well-documented as rising during the middle years."

Must do some grieving for the old self. We do a gut-level reintegration of self, and we face up to our own inevitable death.

"37–42 are the peak years of anxiety for almost everyone."

AGE FRAME	TASKS/ISSUES/KEY QUESTIONS
42–55 **'Renewal or resignation'**	**Key question: What must I do?** **Tasks:** Experience becomes a major tool with which decisions are made. Freedom to be independent, one's own self, within a relationship. No one can totally understand who I am. Parents are forgiven. Children are "released" to be adults. Dealing with aging.
	Key understanding that there is not enough time anymore, so what are my priorities for the time I have left?
	Motto of this stage is "no more bulls--t."
	For men, "the 40s are a time for discovering the emotive parts of themselves that didn't fit with the posture of the strong, dynamic, rational young men they were supposed to be at 25."
	Remember that "middle-aged men and women are the 'norm-bearers and decision-makers,' and that while 'they live in a society … oriented toward youth,' it is 'controlled by the middle-aged' … After 45, most people who have allowed themselves the authenticity crisis are ready to accept entry to middle age and to enjoy its many prerogatives."
	"The crux of it is to see, to feel, and finally to know that none of us can aspire to fulfillment through someone else."

AGE FRAME	TASKS/ISSUES/KEY QUESTIONS
55–70 'Integrity ... despair and disgust'	**Key question:** **What is my legacy?** **What am I going to do next?** **How can I give back?**  **Tasks:** Address career questions. Do I retire or do I stay? If I am forced out of my career, what do I do? If I retire, what will I do next? Health issues. Financial issues: Can I afford to retire? What did/does my life mean? Family commitments and issues—raising grandchildren, etc. More time is devoted to health issues—maintenance, repair, serious illness, etc. According to insurance actuaries, more than one third of individuals who retire are deceased within 18 months. Important to develop new friends—particularly those younger than you. Friends you have had for a long time die. Erikson identified this time as one of gathering greater authenticity for the life lived versus seeing one's life as a mistake, a waste of time, without meaning or purpose. Integrity makes the 70s one of the happiest times for many adults, while others may become trapped in despair and disgust.

7 How Does Adult Development Impact the Classroom and Campus?

tldr: From mentee to mentor, teachers usually grow in stages as well.

20s

- ❏ Very concerned with what they "should" do.
- ❏ Unfamiliar with discipline patterns, response choices, and establishing boundaries. Coaching helps.
- ❏ Very uncertain about how to deal with parents. Helps to have faculty meetings to role-play parent meetings.
- ❏ Benefit significantly from a good mentor.
- ❏ Need to be protected from veteran educators who are rigid and negative.
- ❏ Need good sources of practical advice.

Emotional noise may increase because of uncertainty of patterns and responses.

30s

- Very interested in the latest research. Use it in decision making.
- Need to argue and discuss a new idea before implementation.
- Squeezed by time demands, children, and career advancement.
- Need conversations about career advancement.
- Will pursue advanced degrees.
- After 10 years of teaching, tend to have expertise, and many responses are at the level of automaticity.

Emotional noise may increase because of multiple demands on energy and squeezed time.

 Complete our survey and get a $15 coupon to use in our webstore.
Excludes shipping.
ahaprocess.com/byqt-survey

40s

- ❏ Care about research but will only use it if it makes sense with their experience.
- ❏ Rely upon experience and patterns of response that have worked over time.
- ❏ Extreme fatigue and little patience for "BS."
- ❏ Excellent at being "scouts" for new approaches before they are accepted and implemented.
- ❏ Recognize classroom patterns almost before they start. Experts at preventive approaches.

Emotional noise may be increased by too many changes: "This too will pass." Or a personal crisis may occur that diverts focus and energy.

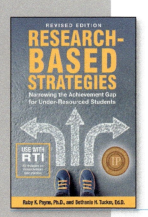

Easily find the interventions you need in the menu-driven *Research-Based Strategies.*

50s

Make excellent mentors.

- ❏ Squeezed by time—aging parents, children returning home, grandchildren issues.
- ❏ Health issues may surface.
- ❏ Slow to implement change if close to retirement.
- ❏ Preoccupation with what comes next.
- ❏ Excellent sounding boards for student analysis and response.
- ❏ For excellent teachers, prowess and expertise becomes phenomenal.

Emotional noise may increase because of squeezed time, less energy, health issues, fatigue with office politics, friends and family who die, etc.

Possible Career Pathways

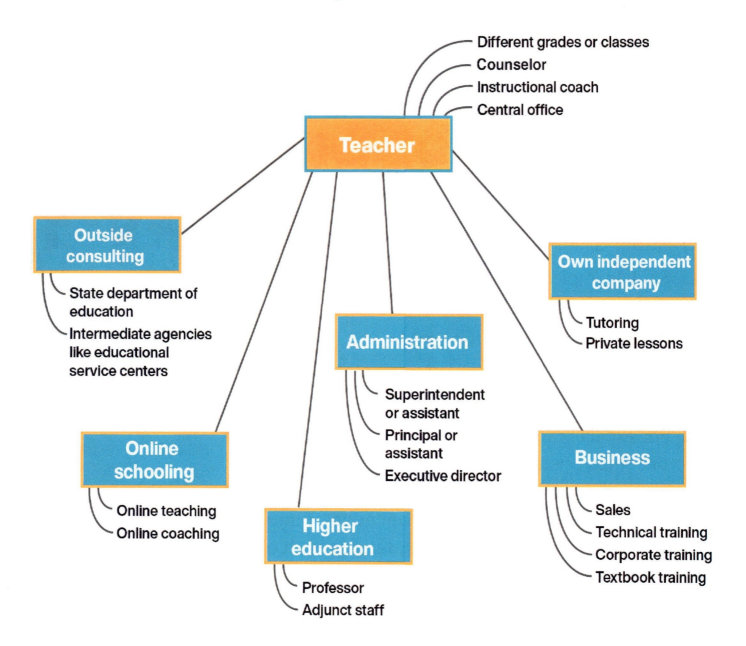

Here Are Some Questions for You to Consider

- What is one thing you would do even if you did not get paid? What do you love to do? What brings you joy?

- What are three experiences you hope to have in your lifetime?

- When you are 100 years old, what do you want people to say about your life?

- What is a talent or skill you have that you can do better than others?

- What is an interest or hobby you have that you would like to pursue?

- If you were ever famous, what would you like to be famous for?

- What is one contribution you could make that would make the world a better place to live?

- What gift do you have? What do you do well that other people do not do as well? What comes almost naturally to you? This is your gift.

For example, one of my gifts is that I can take complex information, simplify it, and then identify a practical way to use the information. It is so easy for me to do that.

8 Value Proposition

tldr:
What value do you bring?
What value do you get?
How do you get purpose, development, coaching, ongoing feedback, and a fulfilling life from your career?

Manage your time closely.

Another part of the larger frame is your value proposition.

A value proposition answers these questions:

What do I bring that has value?
How do I spend my time to get what I value?
What does my employer bring to me that has value to me?

Ruby Payne
Value Proposition: What Do You Bring, What Do You Get?

1. **What do my friends find of value in me?**
   Why do they like to be with me?
   What value do I bring to them? Fun?
   Interesting conversation? Help?
   A listening ear? Entertainment?
   Thoughtfulness? Caring? New ideas?
   A shared hobby? A shared experience?

2. **What value do your friends/family bring to you?**

Full resources/videos available at *ahaprocess.com/byqt*

3. **What do I bring to teaching that has value?**
   In all companies/institutions, there is some sort of bottom line. In a company, it is profits. You cannot stay in business if you do not have profits. In the school business, it is student achievement and growth. What value do you bring to your students and your campus? Why would they want to keep you?

4. **What value does your school, administration, and employer bring to you?**
   A paycheck? Meaningful work? Good colleagues? Flexibility?

This is the value proposition. Why is it important? If you want to get what you hope for out of life, you have to know the value you bring to work and family/friends AND the value they bring to you.

This Gallup piece about the changing world of work lays out what the employer brings to the younger worker that has value versus what employers offered in the past.

The Change in Leadership

PAST ➡ FUTURE

- ❏ My paycheck
- ❏ My satisfaction
- ❏ My boss
- ❏ My annual review
- ❏ My weaknesses
- ❏ My job

- ❏ My purpose
- ❏ My development
- ❏ My coach
- ❏ My ongoing conversations
- ❏ My strengths
- ❏ My life

If the Future Values Are Important to You, How Do You Get That in Your Employment?

What you value determines how you spend your time to a great extent.

The second part of a value proposition is TIME. If the future values are valuable to me, or to my friends/family, or to my employer, how do I get all of that with the TIME that I have? Everyone has only 24 hours a day.

Here is how to look at how you spend your time: For a week, record what you do with your time every hour. How much time do you spend on social media, at work, driving, sleeping, etc.?

It will give you a sense of where your time is going. One of the things I did not know in my 20s was how very important TIME is. It is the one thing that you cannot recapture, and it is the one thing that you cannot make more of.

> **If you want to get what you hope for out of life, you have to know the value you bring to work and family/friends AND the value they bring to you.**

Once you have an idea of where your time is going, you can decide if that is where you want it to go.

If you keep track of your time for a week, you will recognize how much time you actually "waste." For productive people, time is their most valuable commodity.

For a week, use this time sheet to break down how you are spending your time every day, every hour.

Sunday	Monday	Tuesday	Wednesday	Thursday	Friday	Saturday

9 Future Story

tldr: You need a story of your future, and if teaching isn't in it, you need to find a different career. A visual story board is a good way to make a future story.

To get what you hope for requires a plan. That plan is called a future story. If teaching does not fall into your future story, then you should get out. You will be miserable, and your employer will be miserable. If you are not sure, then continue to teach for a year or two, and when you reevaluate, you will know.

Every four or five years, I have my employees do a future story, and I ask to see it. If the work they do for me is not in that future story, then I encourage them to look for work elsewhere. I want them to be happy and fulfilled.

Work takes at least eight hours a day, and if you aren't spending those eight hours a day doing something fulfilling, there are other professions you can try.

**Why do you want a future story?
If you don't have one, someone else will determine what your life story is.**

- ❏ I have a future story.
- ❏ I redo mine every year.
- ❏ I change what is important to me as I get older. I have done it for years. This is the fastest way I know to determine your future story.
- ❏ Make a box with nine squares.
- ❏ Label the squares like the ones in the image (next pages).
- ❏ Put a picture in each box. These pictures represent what you would like to have/do/be by the time you are 35.
- ❏ When you are finished with this, print it off.
- ❏ Put it where you can see it every day.
- ❏ Relax.
- ❏ Don't stress yourself about it.

You will be amazed how much of it actually happens for you.

Ruby Payne
Building Your Future Story

> **W**hy do you want a future story? If you don't have one, someone else will determine what your life story is.

Another degree or certificate you eventually want to have	The unique gift you have (meaning) and how you will share it (purpose)	A career path that you want to pursue— what you will look like as an educator
Relationship/ significant other/ marriage	What your financial situation will be	Where you will live
Things you will do for fun	Children/family/pets	Hobbies, groups to which you belong, causes you support, church you belong to

Another way to get a future story is to use the Mind Movies app to make a movie of it.

Full resources/videos available at *ahaprocess.com/byqt*

Sample Visual Story Board

Master's Degree	Purpose and Meaning	Work—what you love to do and would do even if you did not get paid
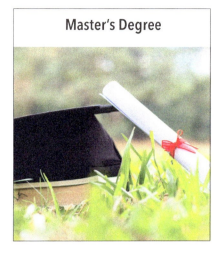	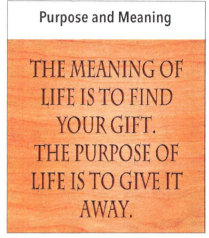	
Car/Vehicle	Pay/Money	House/Apartment
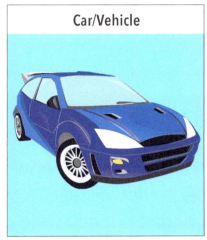	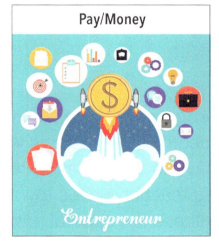	
Friends	Relationship/Marriage	Fun/Hobby
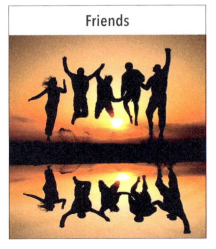		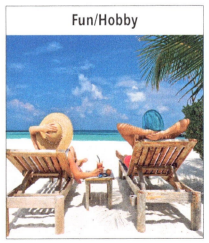

10 Self-Assessment

tldr: To take control of your life and your journey as a teacher, you need to take continual stock of yourself. Use the subsequent expert teacher rubric to establish benchmarks and work toward the goal of becoming an expert teacher.

Are you progressing and learning? In addition to having a mentor and someone who can "coach" you, you also have to self-assess. I have a rubric here of how a beginning teacher moves toward expertise. Please remember these are general patterns, and not everyone will follow the patterns exactly. They are a bit like a map drawn on the back of an envelope. They give you an idea of the direction you want to go. The research shows that male brains tend to overestimate their abilities, and female brains tend to underestimate their abilities. Because of these tendencies, it is important to self-assess. It is your journey and your life, and self-assessment will keep you on track.

Ruby Payne
Self-Assessment for Teachers

Expert Teacher Rubric

	Beginning	Developing	Capable	Expert
Safe, culturally competent learning environment	Little classroom management. No clear procedures. Has favorite students and ignores others. Engages in negative comments about students during class. Many discipline referrals. May blur physical or verbal boundaries.	Classroom is usually calm, with procedures and discipline established. Some relational aggression between students. Cultural differences not always understood. Helps students when requested. Boundaries are generally appropriate and intact.	Establishes mutual respect in classroom (support, insistence, high expectations). Calm, businesslike atmosphere. Classroom is relational and inclusive. Actively ensures student well-being.	Rapport with nearly every student. Positive regard for competency, culture, and individuality of each student. Gets best from students. Students have great respect for teacher. Addresses emotional issues appropriately.
Student achievement	Gives formative assessments but doesn't use results for decision making in instruction. May blame students for not learning. Assignments often not on grade level. Doesn't know value of relationships in learning. Doesn't know names of many students.	Gives feedback and correctives on student work. Most assignments on grade level. Has relationships of respect with some students. May work with individual students to augment their instructional needs. Slow to pick up on needs of highly mobile students. Knows most students' names.	Know where they want each student by end of year. Can discuss each student with some accuracy by name and achievement characteristics. Welcomes questions from students and quickly assesses new students for achievement levels. Most students are in top two quartiles.	By end of first month of school, has an accurate assessment of individual achievement needs of each student. Daily tailors group and individual instruction to get phenomenal growth from EACH student. Takes students to new levels of competence and promotes their growth.

Expert Teacher Rubric

	Beginning	Developing	Capable	Expert
Content expertise (purpose, structure, patterns, processes)	Limited understanding of content. Cannot sort important from unimportant.	Heavily dependent on textbooks, curriculum assists, etc. Unable to clearly explain content and translate to students' understandings.	Good understanding of content. Clearly explains it with stories, examples, drawings, mental models. Processes clearly taught. Knows when students are confused versus totally wrong.	Extraordinary understanding of content. Frames it so students can understand quickly. Teaches both conceptually and in great detail. Students often develop additional interest in content.
Student intervention and diagnosis	Says, "I treat them all the same." Makes few adjustments for individual students. Unable to assess what would work with individual students. Many failures.	Interventions used but not necessarily successful. Accuracy of student performance limited. Often will say, "I don't know what to do." Tends to be surprised by student failures.	Quick, accurate intervention and diagnosis. Doesn't wait for students to fail. Will seek support for students from multiple sources. Some failures.	Often uses preventive interventions before students can falter or become discouraged. Almost always intervenes accurately. Few failures.
Teaching performance	Lots of "busy work." Instruction disconnected. Much "what" instruction but very little "how" and "why." Teaching is done "to" students, not "with" them.	Instructional design is solid but fails to engage many of the students. Pedagogy is limited. Gaps in explanation. Little "why" in instruction. Has difficulty monitoring group and individuals. May get sidetracked.	Lesson is connected to most students' interests. Varied pedagogy. Opportunity to question and interact with teacher. Teacher monitors both group as a whole and individuals within group simultaneously.	There's flow to instruction (regardless of pedagogy)—seamless, almost effortless but exceedingly effective. Individually and collectively, students are engaged. Relaxed yet intense approach to learning. Students leave wanting to know more. Humor is often part of instruction.

Full resources/videos available at ahaprocess.com/byqt

Expert Teacher Rubric

	Beginning	Developing	Capable	Expert
Paperwork, organizational and legal responsibilities, professional ethics	Misses deadlines frequently. Not cognizant of legal implications of decisions. Often must be prompted about paperwork. Grading procedures, standards compliance, etc. are questionable. Creates difficulties with other staff and administration.	Meets most deadlines. Is aware of most legal implications and responds appropriately. Grades and other paperwork are accurate. Tolerated but not necessarily respected by other staff.	Paperwork and organization are good. Grades are accurate and careful. Responsibilities, including legal, are addressed. Professional ethics are invariably present. Is generally respected by other staff.	Paperwork completed. Virtually always organized and legal. Highly respected by other staff members, even if they don't agree. Grades are respected. Works to create better staff relationships. Asset to campus and community.
Parental contact and interaction	Blames parents or avoids parents. Little predictable communication with them. Often condescending to or defensive with parents during conferences.	Contacts parents if there is difficulty with student. Other communication with parents is limited. In conferencing, lectures more than dialogs. Doesn't see it as partnership.	Sees parents as potential partners to help student. Has regular communication with parents. Adjusts without judgment for limitations of some parents.	Highly regarded by parents in community. Often requested as teacher. Works to create partnership with parents. Communicates regularly and appropriately.

It is your journey and your life, and self-assessment will keep you on track.

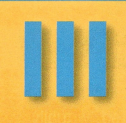

11 The Daily Stressors and Frustrations: How to Deal with Them

tldr: Stress comes from every direction. There are many myths about teaching. Adjusting your expectations can help reduce stress. Failure to reduce stress can manifest as psychological symptoms.

Stressors come from the following: unrealistic expectations, losing perspective, and inadequate tools and solutions to lower the stress.

> The first part of dealing with frustrations is to have a realistic set of expectations.

You won't leave teaching because you don't love to teach. If you do leave teaching, it will be because of the frustrations in teaching. If you hear yourself using the word "should" too much, as in, "The student/administrator/system SHOULD…" then you are in an argument with reality.

The first part of dealing with frustrations is to have a realistic set of expectations. For example, if you live in any big city, and you expect to get to work in 10 minutes via the freeway, you need to rethink your expectations. It is the same in the school business. Here are some common myths and corresponding realities.

Myth	Reality
All students are motivated to learn if the teacher is excellent. 	All students are motivated to learn, but they are NOT necessarily motivated to learn WHAT YOU TEACH. Some students couldn't care less about school, do not want to be there, and cannot be motivated without individualized interventions. Some students have so much instability outside school that they come only for food, safety, and warmth, not necessarily to learn. Sometimes a student simply has no interest in what you are teaching, and nothing you try will work. It is okay if you don't reach every single student. This is a hard job, and you will experience failures. The important thing is to learn from them and move on.
Parents want to partner with the teacher for the best educational opportunity for their child.	Many parents are overwhelmed by life, work two jobs, are parenting alone, and do not want to work with you. These parents are doing the best they can, but they are probably not going to call you back. Your call is simply one more aggravation in their day. Many parents are not going to support you at all—particularly when it comes to discipline.
The public school system is set up to help students learn and be successful. 	The school system's focus is not necessarily on student learning and student success. School districts are legal entities set up to make sure every student in a geographic area between the ages of 5 and 18 has the opportunity to go to school. Laws governing the school system are made by individuals and institutions who are far removed from the classroom. The public school system is a necessary institution for a democracy. For students from poverty, it is one of the biggest sources of hope and/or despair in their lives.

Myth	Reality
My principal will support nme and help me deal with difficult students and parents	The principal is not God and has only 24 hours a day. The principal does not have an unlimited budget. Principals often have to answer to central office and state directives that they have no control over. Principals right now are mostly crisis managers unless they are in highly resourced schools. Principals have uneven strengths and weaknesses. Some do not have the skills or training to be in the role of principal, but they keep their jobs because they are able to maintain some order and safety.
Other veteran teachers will help me.	Veteran teachers are overwhelmed also, and they may or may not have time to help you—or even to offer you advice. If your campus does not have a system for teaming or professional learning communities, you will need to find a source outside your campus for support.
I will be given a reasonable workload and number of preps. I will get to teach in my area of expertise.	You will have to teach outside your area, and you will have more responsibilities and more students than you anticipated. Particularly in middle and high schools, new teachers are asked to teach one or two classes outside their area of content expertise. It is not unusual that a new teacher will have five preps per day.
The school district will make good administrative and policy decisions.	Not all the time. The school district is governed by elected or appointed board members who are removed from the day-to-day life of the school. They have been elected to protect/advocate for certain constituencies. They may or may not know much about education, read their board minutes, or stay informed. They may be intrusive, taking

Myth	Reality
	incredible amounts of time from administrators for their issues. They usually do not get paid to do the job, and very few people call them to tell them they are doing a good job. Being a board member is a thankless job. If there are difficult board members or an incompetent superintendent, then it is difficult to have a system that is well-governed.
I will get good, frequent feedback about my teaching.	Probably not. Who has the time to give all that feedback? When I was a principal, I had 500 students in my building, no assistant, and 40 staff members. I gave more feedback to new teachers than veterans, but I would have loved to have more time to do a better job of giving feedback to all the teachers.
In my first year of teaching, I will "get my feet wet."	In your first year, you will most likely be dumped in headfirst with no life jacket. The first year is all about SURVIVAL.
My family and friends will understand my fatigue and lack of work-life balance.	Not always. Family and friends may be understanding at first, but over time, the long hours and stressful conditions can spill over into other areas of your life and affect relationships. Ask these people to revisit the value of high-quality teachers in their schools and to advocate for better conditions in education overall.
I will have a heated and air-conditioned classroom with quality desks and modern equipment.	Not necessarily. You may get the room that none of the veteran teachers wanted—and you'll find out why. It may or may not have desks, shelves, or tech equipment. Particularly if you are in a school that serves students from poverty, you may find that your classroom presents some challenges before the students ever arrive.

Myth	Reality
I will get clear directives and guidance about curriculum, instruction, and testing.	If your school is underperforming, then curriculum, instruction, and testing are most likely implemented poorly, haphazardly, or too rigidly. Support is likely mixed, and directives are often unclear.
I will be able to meet my own expectations of excellent teaching.	For your first two years of teaching, your goal is survival. Any progress you make toward excellence is a bonus. The main question is: Can you cover the basics? Don't worry. It won't be like this forever. But in the first two years, the goal is to get the basics down and THEN start the improvement process.
The school system will provide classroom materials.	Not necessarily. In a high-poverty district, it is very unlikely.
I will be able to handle the emotional issues of students. 	One of the hardest realities of being a teacher or administrator is the way some children are treated outside of school. It is quite simply heartbreaking. If you remain a caring and committed teacher or administrator, you never get over it. But you do learn to put it in perspective and realize you cannot save every student.
The politics and policies of the school district will not bother me. I will close my door and teach.	WRONG. They WILL bother you because they will impact your teaching and your students. You have to figure out what is in your circle of concern versus your circle of influence. (See *The 7 Habits of Highly Effective People* for more.)
I will be able to "figure out" all my students and find ways to get them to work with me.	You will be able to figure out most of them and find workable solutions, but in the course of your career you will have a few students you will never forget. They are the ones who haunt you because you were unable to find a solution that worked for you both.

Stress impacts your mental, emotional, and physical health.

In the research, these are listed as the primary sources of stress for new teachers:

- ❏ work overload
- ❏ lack of support from teachers
- ❏ lack of support from administrators
- ❏ discipline challenges
- ❏ curriculum challenges
- ❏ work demands
- ❏ family demands
- ❏ wanting to meet self-expectations
- ❏ lack of set routines
- ❏ classroom time management
- ❏ not having clear expectations

Ruby Payne Daily Stressors and Frustrations

When our system gets stressed, it often shows up as psychological symptoms.

PSYCHOLOGICAL SYMPTOMS OF STRESS

HYSTERICS — INSOMNIA — HEADACHE — DEPRESSION — ANGER

12 Tools to De-Stress

tldr: Manage self-talk. Use tapping techniques. Reframe negative situations. Escape and stay out of dramatic triangles where sometimes you're the victim, sometimes you're the rescuer, and sometimes you're the bully. Maintain a long view, and reframe failures into opportunities for successful learning.

Ruby Payne
Tools for Teachers to De-Stress

Full resources/videos available at *ahaprocess.com/byqt*

Eliminate Negative Self-Talk

Manage your self-talk
Your self-talk is that back door you have into your brain that conveys negative messages and doubt. It might say things like:

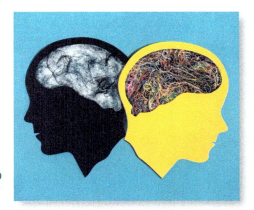

1. This is stupid. This will never happen. Why try?
2. Remember those last three failures you had? Why would this one be any different?
3. You will never be as good as she is. Why try?
4. You don't have enough time. You don't have enough money.

How do you manage that self-talk?
Here are some questions to ask yourself:

1. What is the worst thing that could happen if this does not work out? Will I be exactly where I am right now?
2. What will people say about me? (That is their problem, not yours.)
3. Is that actually true? Identify two times when it was not true.
4. Will it make a difference in five years?
5. Who will probably support me in this venture?
6. Will I stagnate even more if I do not do this? Will I lose a part of myself if I do not try this?

Tapping
One of the fastest ways to calm your stress levels is a technique called tapping from thought-field therapy. The late Roger Callahan laid out this technique in a book called *Tapping the Healer Within.*

Protocol

Step One: Identify an issue and assign a number
Identify the issue/fear that is bothering you.
Give it a number on a scale of 1–10 (10 is high).

Step Two: The setup
Even though I have this _____ (fear or issue), I deeply and completely accept myself.

Say the above statement three times and do the karate chop (KC).

Step Three: Tapping
EB (eyebrows), SE (side of eye), UE (under eye), UN (under nose), CH (chin), CB (collarbone), UA (under the arm), BN (below the nipple), TH (thumb), IF (index finger), MF (middle finger), BF (baby finger), KC (karate chop).

EB, SE, UE, UN, CH, CB, UA, BN, TH, IF, MF, BF, KC

Step Four: The gamut
While tapping on the top of the hand between the little finger and the next finger, do the following:

Eyes open, eyes closed, eyes down hard to the right while holding the hand steady, eyes down hard to the left while holding the hand steady, roll the eyes in a circle, roll the eyes in a circle in the opposite direction, hum two seconds of a song, count from 1 to 5 quickly, hum two seconds of a song.

Step Five: Check number from STEP ONE; if the number is not down to zero, say this:
Even though I still have some of this _____ (fear or issue), I deeply and completely accept myself.

Then repeat the process (steps 2–5).

Reframing

Reframing is a technique used to identify the behavior that will be compatible with identity. It requires the adult voice. It doesn't work if the person has a biochemical issue or addiction, and it must be framed against the individual's identity. An example is physical fighting.

Many students physically fight because it is seen as a position of strength. If you reframe it this way—"It takes more strength to stay out of a fight than to get into one"—you have reframed it. When parents tell me that they have told their child to fight, I thank them for giving the child necessary survival skills for their environment.

Then I ask them this question: "Do you fight at work?" What you are trying to get the parent to see is that there is an appropriate place to physically fight, and it isn't school or work.

Statements to help reframe a situation include:

- This behavior (not fighting) will help you win more often.
- This will keep you from being cheated.
- This will help you be tougher or stronger.
- This will make you smarter.
- This will help keep the people you love safe.
- This will give you power, control, and respect.
- This will keep you safer.

A coach south of Houston told me this story:
The coaches had a rule that anyone who was late to class owed them a minute of pushups for every minute late. A 10th-grade boy was late. The coach said, "Give me a minute of pushups."

The boy said "No way." The boy got sent to the office and received 45 minutes of detention.

The next day the coach said to the boy, "I didn't understand why you gave up a minute for 45 minutes." The boy was confused. So the coach said, "Yesterday, you could have done a minute of pushups, but you chose 45 minutes of detention. I didn't understand."

The day after that the boy came to the coach and said, "I'll do pushups next time." The coach had reframed the situation not as power and control but as use of time.

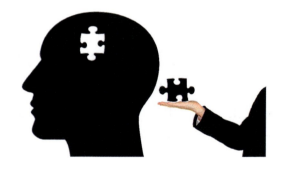

See failure as a learning opportunity.

Are You in a Triangle?

Development of appropriate boundaries

Emotional resources additionally are linked to appropriate boundaries. Boundaries signify the ability to say "no" to being "used." In other words, boundaries allow you to maintain self-respect. The closer you get to survival, the fewer the boundaries.

Spaces are crowded, resources are scarce, one has to "give" in order to "get." These factors over time lead to abuse, manipulation, codependence, and servitude.

The response to a lack of boundaries frequently is to become over-controlling, manipulative, and fixated. Options are seldom considered, and thinking becomes polarized; it's "either/or." Psychologists also call this "black or white thinking."

The easiest way to start this discussion in the classroom is to identify physical boundaries:

- How much space in the room is actually theirs?
- How do you keep someone out of your space?
- How do you stay in your space?

This discussion of physical boundaries is the beginning of setting emotional boundaries.

To establish boundaries, it's important to understand the Karpman triangle.

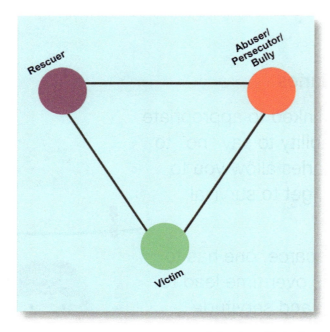

Karpman Triangle

The same person can take on all three roles in different situations. In one setting the person is a bully, in another setting the person is a rescuer, and in another setting the person is a victim. Once you are in the triangle, you will eventually take on all three roles—and boundaries disappear because ownership isn't taken by anyone. To stay out of the triangle, you can ask questions.

Here's an example of using questions to avoid the triangle.

When my son was in second grade, he came home from school and told me he was "bored." I asked him, "Whose problem is that?"

He said, "The teacher's." He was presenting himself as a victim and asking me to go to school and "rescue" him.

I asked him, "Is the teacher bored?"

He said, "No, I am."

I said, "Then it isn't the teacher's problem. It's your problem. Since it's your problem, how can you solve it?"

Had I gone to the school and "bullied" the teacher in order to "rescue" my son who was a "victim," chances are that the teacher would've felt like a "victim" and gone to the principal to be "rescued."

The principal likely would've called me and "bullied" me for being so insensitive to the teacher and blaming the teacher for my son's problems. And then I would have felt like a "victim" and told my husband so that he would "rescue" me and go to school and "bully" the principal. The cycle would continue.

In other words, once a person is in the triangle, that person can be expected to take on all three roles eventually. Most importantly, the problem won't get solved, and boundaries will disappear. The best way to stay out of the triangle is to ask questions and clarify the issues so that the problem can be solved.

See failure as a learning opportunity:
It took Edison many tries to get a light bulb to work. When asked about it, he said he knew thousands of ways that DID NOT work!

> **W**hat is the significance of this in time?
> **W**ill it matter in one year?
> **W**ill it matter in five years?

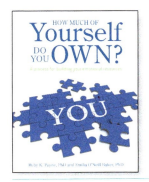

Find more self-awareness exercises that Ruby found helpful in her own life.

How Much of Yourself Do You Own? A Process for Building Your Emotional Resources

13 Resources, Solutions, and Insights to Help You Stay in Teaching If You Are in a High-Poverty School

tldr: You are different from your students, but making an effort to understand them will build relationships that foster learning.

If you teach in a high-poverty school, the salary and stability your job provides puts you in a different economic class than most of your students.

Even if you grew up in the same neighborhood as some of your students, going to college and becoming a teacher creates a gap that can be difficult to close.

Trying to understand and empathize with your students—while keeping in mind you can never understand totally—will show them that you care and will form the basis for relationships of mutual respect.

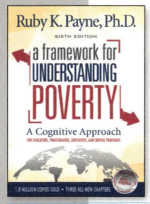

Have you read the new sixth edition of *A Framework for Understanding Poverty* with three all-new chapters?

A Framework for Understanding Poverty: A Cognitive Approach, Sixth Edition

Full resources/videos available at *ahaprocess.com/byqt*

Don't know where to start when trying to walk a mile in their shoes?

The following insights should help, and they lead naturally into classroom management strategies that can reduce your discipline referrals and make your classroom a place where everyone succeeds.

14 Students

tldr: Many students are in school for food and socializing only; they are not there to learn. Some DO want to learn, but hidden rules and realities of poverty can create barriers. Intersectionality impacts relationships and learning. Points of intersection with poverty include race, gender, immigration, language learning, homelessness, and more. Rural and urban poverty have similarities and differences.

The very first thing to know about students from poverty is that many of the students do not come to school to learn. They come for food or to be warm or to be safe. In the U.S., 3.2 million people live on $1.90 a day. And another 5.3 million live on $4.00 a day.

When 11.5 million children in the U.S. have food insecurity, and many of them do not eat on the weekends, you can be sure many students COME TO SCHOOL FOR FOOD.

It is very important to be AUTHENTIC.

Full resources/videos available at *ahaprocess.com/byqt*

It is hard to concentrate and learn when you are hungry. Try it yourself. Go for a day without eating and see what effect it has on your basic cognition. You may be surprised!

The point is that the expectation that everyone comes to school to learn is not realistic. Some students come because they have to come—otherwise they are truant. Even among the students who DO want to learn, not everyone is ready to learn that day. If they didn't get much sleep, if they are hungry, if they are stressed because they have to move again, learning may not be a priority. Learning may not even be possible until other needs are met.

Your students also probably have different "hidden rules" from the ones you are used to. Hidden rules are unspoken cueing mechanisms that individuals/groups use to know whether a person belongs or not. Your grandmother had hidden rules about her house. There are hidden rules by

religion, by region of the country, by country of origin, by race, by gender, by age, by occupation, etc. There are hidden rules by class also. Not everyone in the group may use the hidden rules, but if you know hidden rules, you understand why behaviors occur.

For example, in poverty or survival environments, some of the rules you may use are these:

❏ Laugh or smirk when you are disciplined,

❏ Spend money on entertainment because it takes away the pain (e.g., student has a new phone but no paper or pencil),

❏ Give up achievement for a relationship,

❏ Talk back to the teacher because being tough gets you respect,

❏ Don't work for teachers if you don't like them, etc.

For more information on hidden rules, see Chapter 3 in *A Framework for Understanding Poverty*.

Your students' external environment is often very unstable and chaotic. Nothing is predictable. Resources are thin, so a person learns not to plan. Many students and parents from poverty do not plan. They do not use calendars. They do not use clocks. They often keep time based on what is on television. Transportation, housing, work, and food are all unpredictable. Tasks like getting homework done, getting to school on time, sitting up and paying attention when they were up half the night—**none of this is going to happen unless you teach it.**

**Podcast:
Maintaining your emotional stability when students lose theirs**

When the external environment is unstable and chaotic, it becomes harder to control your emotional responses. You learn to react. It helps you survive. Most of the discipline referrals, nonreaders, dropouts, and special education students are male.

One of the reasons is that 76% of teachers in K–12 are female, but 50% of the student population is male. Male and female brains have differences chemically, structurally, and in how they process information and emotions. Male brains typically take more time to process an emotional incident. Female brains tend to process emotions more quickly. For more information about this, please see Chapter 5 in *Emotional Poverty*.

> **They come for food or to be warm or to be safe.**

The greater the number of students from poverty, the greater the number of students identified as special education or in need of an IEP or 504 plan. The Individuals with Disabilities Education Act is a federal law that requires that adaptations be made for these students' learning.

The current process is called RTI—Response to Intervention. Rather than wait for students to fail before an intervention is made, the intervention must be made at the first indication that there is a learning or behavioral issue.

For a new teacher, trying to identify interventions that work can be frustrating. In my book *Research-Based Strategies*, there is a checklist of strategies that can be used when a student needs intervention.

In a high-poverty school, you will have immigrant students and English language learners.

There tend to be more of these students in high-poverty schools because those schools are located in low-income neighborhoods where marginalized people can afford to live. There are both cultural and language issues for these students.

Another factor is whether they are first-generation immigrants, second-generation, or third-generation. First-generation immigrants tend to rely heavily on the culture of their native country. Parents keep the native language. Their children often feel torn between the culture of their parents and the demands of U.S. cultural norms.

Easily find the interventions you need in the menu-driven *Research-Based Strategies.*

Maria Montaño-Harmon found that if immigrants are still in a high-poverty neighborhood by the third generation, the adults have less formal register in any language than their ancestors who emigrated in the first place. She found that the issue for many immigrants is that they know only casual register in English and in their native language.

For an in-depth discussion, please see *A Framework for Understanding Poverty*.

There seem to be four factors that impact the ability of immigrants to negotiate school and work in the USA.

These four factors are:
- ❏ How well they speak English,
- ❏ The amount of trauma they suffered in the immigration process,
- ❏ Whether or not there is a support system of individuals from the native country,
- ❏ The level of education attained in the native country.

The more educated the individual, the more fluent they are in English, the less trauma they suffered in the immigration process, and the greater the support system of individuals from their native country, the easier the process of immigration is. The easiest way to assess the educational level of the parents is to ask how many years they went to school. **As a general rule, the more years they went to school, the better educated they will be.**

In a high-poverty school, you will have more culturally and linguistically marginalized students, because while 62% of all people in poverty in America are white, people of color have much larger percentages of individuals in poverty; i.e., marginalized groups are disproportionately represented among all people in poverty. Depending on the area of the country you are in, the marginalized groups you have on your campus will be different.

If you are a white teacher teaching in a school where the majority of the students are from marginalized groups, there will often be an immediate distrust of you. The history of racial discrimination in particular feeds and exacerbates this distrust, but there are ways to overcome that to some extent and build relationships of trust and mutual respect.

If you are a teacher in a high-poverty district, especially one with a large population of culturally and linguistically marginalized students, it is very important to be AUTHENTIC. Accept the fact that you will not understand all of your students' experiences. Don't pretend to understand. If they distrust you because of your race, don't argue with them. Your students will respect you when they know that you care.

Homeless students are growing in number. Some homeless students "couch surf"; i.e., they move from one friend's or relative's house to the next. Some families live in their cars. Some are on the street or in shelters. To help homeless students, please remember the following:

a) It will be difficult for them to stay organized. If you are moving constantly, you have no place to put your personal items, and organization is almost impossible. Provide students who need one a place in your classroom where they can keep their papers, notebooks, etc.

b) Depending on how crowded or unstable the housing was the night before, there may be lost sleep and difficulty concentrating/focusing the next day in school.

c) Refrain from asking personal questions. Many times, homeless students do not know what the reality will be that day or later that evening.

d) Find out if they need food. Students who are hungry have trouble being at their best in the classroom.

e) Remember how difficult it is to keep an even emotional keel when there is nothing predictable in your life—not even food or sleep.

When a person is focused on survival, there are some universal experiences: difficulty planning, the need to react, hypervigilance about people (some are safe and some are not), the need to be able to physically defend oneself, etc. However, there are some differences between rural and urban poverty that are worth talking about.

Rural poverty tends to be more isolated, transportation is more problematic, there is more incest, and last names are known in the rural community. It is almost a caste system instead of a class system in rural communities. Often, because of guilt by association, any member of a family with a bad reputation is written off automatically. Rural communities also tend to have more suicides.

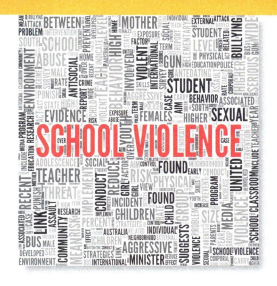

Urban poverty, on the other hand, has more homicides, more sexual abuse by individuals who are not related by blood, and more access to transportation and the Internet. There is more gang-related activity in urban poverty.

Urban and rural poverty both have high levels of drug use and violence, high teen pregnancy rates, lower levels of marriage, and a higher percentage of households without fathers. Adults in urban and rural poverty are less-educated, and the jobs available tend to be less than full-time and/or sporadic. There are more preventable deaths in households in poverty than in educated households. Men in poverty die on the average 10 years younger than their peers in educated households.

Podcast:
Neighborhood effects and secondary students

15 Discipline and Classroom Management

tldr: Students and teachers may have different ideas about discipline. A highly structured classroom with clear, predefined procedures can reduce the need for discipline interventions. Introducing a competitive element to classroom management can motivate students to behave.

Discipline and classroom management can be especially challenging issues for teachers who grew up in middle class and now teach in high-poverty schools. Not only do the students have different hidden rules than these teachers, the typical middle class approaches to discipline are often ineffective.

In middle class households, the purpose of discipline is to change behavior. In households in generational poverty, the understanding is that you cannot change who you are. Discipline is about punishment and forgiveness, not about change. This means the idea that discipline is supposed to change behavior is a new idea for many students.

Classroom management/procedures checklist

In high-poverty schools, you have to have a very structured classroom management process because the students often live in chaotic environments. My book *Working with Students* has detailed classroom management procedures broken down by grade level: K–2, 3–5, 6–8, and 9–12. You also need to know that classes have "personalities." You have to work with the personality of the class, as well as with individual behaviors. *Working with Students* contains a discussion of classroom personalities.

Finally, many discipline problems are rooted in deep emotional issues that traditional discipline strategies do not address.

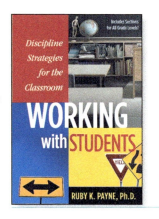

Benefit by seeing classroom procedures from experienced teachers at all levels.

Working with Students: Discipline Strategies for the Classroom

See my book *Emotional Poverty* for strategies to create a classroom that reduces anger, anxiety, and violence.

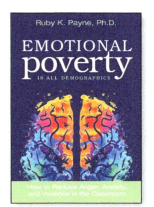

Learn how to identify and address insecure, emotionally unbonded students.

Emotional Poverty in All Demographics

PROCEDURES CHECKLIST

The following list is adapted from "Guidelines for the First Days of School" from the Research Development Center for Teacher Education, Research on Classrooms, University of Texas, Austin.

Starting class

Taking attendance

Marking absences

Tardy students

Giving makeup work for absentees

Enrolling new students

Un-enrolling students

Students who have to leave school early

Warm-up activity (that students begin as soon as they walk into classroom)

My procedure

PROCEDURES CHECKLIST

Instructional time

Student movement within classroom

Use of phones and headphones

Student movement in and out of classroom

Going to restroom

Getting students' attention

Students talking during class

What students do when their work is completed

Working together as group(s)

Handing in papers/homework

Appropriate headings for papers

Bringing/distributing/using textbooks

Leaving room for special class

Students who don't have paper and/or pencils

Signal(s) for getting student attention

Touching other students in classroom

Eating food in classroom

Laboratory procedures (materials and supplies, safety routines, cleaning up)

Students who get sick during class

Using pencil sharpener

Listing assignments/homework/due dates

Systematically monitoring student learning during instruction

My procedure

 Download your own fill-in-the-blank procedure document

PROCEDURES CHECKLIST

Ending class

Putting things away

Dismissing class

Collecting papers and assignments

My procedure

Other

Lining up for lunch/recess/special events

Walking to lunch/recess

Putting away coats and backpacks

Cleaning out locker

Preparing for fire drills and/or bomb threats

Going to gym for assemblies/pep rallies

Respecting teacher's desk and storage areas

Appropriately handling/using computers/equipment

My procedure

PROCEDURES CHECKLIST

Student accountability

Late work

Missing work

Extra credit

Redoing work and/or retaking tests

Incomplete work

Neatness

Papers with no names

Using pens, pencils, colored markers

Using computer-generated products

Internet access on computers

Setting and assigning due dates

Writing on back of paper

Makeup work and amount of time for makeup work

Use of mobile devices, headphones during class

Letting students know assignments missed during absence

Percentage of grade for major tests, homework, etc.

Explaining your grading policy

Letting new students know your procedures

Having contact with all students at least once during week

Exchanging papers

Using Internet for posting assignments and sending them in

My procedure

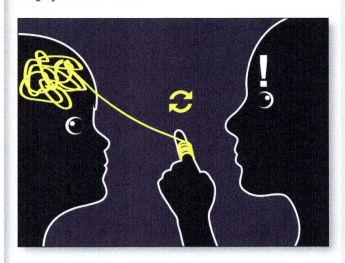

Download your own fill-in-the-blank procedure document

PROCEDURES CHECKLIST

How will you…?

Determine grades on report cards (components and weights of those components)?

Grade daily assignments?

Record grades so that assignments and dates are included?

Have students keep records of their own grades?

Make sure your assignments and grading reflect progress against standards?

Notify parents when students are not passing or are having other academic problems?

Contact parents if a problem arises regarding student behavior?

Keep records and documentation of student behavior?

Document adherence to IEP (individualized education plan)?

Return graded papers in a timely manner?

Monitor students who have serious health issues (peanut allergies, diabetes, epilepsy, etc.)?

My procedure

A few rules to remember for classrooms with a high number of students from poverty:

1. Discipline that "takes things away" from students rarely works. They have had so many things taken away from them that it doesn't matter. Furthermore, if your discipline strategy is to take away privileges, what do you do with the students who lose all their privileges in the first 10 minutes of class?

2. Positive rewards work to get a behavior started. Once the behavior is started, however, you have to reassign the rewards to other behaviors. To continue with the rewards for the same behavior after it's established actually decreases the behavior.

3. Relational, competitive behavior systems tend to work; i.e., working with one other person in a team of two fosters a relationship and friendly competition that leads to success. For example, I know a seventh-grade teacher who made a poster of a football field to hang on the wall, and then he put the students into teams. Each team had a football with the logo of a college that they wanted to attend. To move the ball across the field, he had a list of how to make yards (good behaviors), how to lose yards (bad behavior), and how to make a touchdown (really good behavior). Each day the footballs would move, and each week, one team would win. Rewards were given. Then the teams were shuffled and reset. This relational, competitive activity added a lot of order to the classroom because the students really wanted to win.

Ruby Payne and Rita Pierson
Three Voices Demo

16 Parents: Why Don't They Come to Events Like Parent-Teacher Conferences? Don't They Care?

tldr: Parents from poverty probably won't trust you right away. Understanding the reasons for this and being true to yourself will help you gain trust and respect. Keep communication about events and other needs simple and straightforward. The parenting style in poverty may surprise you; keep in mind that it is motivated by love for the children.

Ask Ruby:
What Do You Do When You Cannot Get Ahold of a Parent?

Many parents from poverty had a bad experience in school. For people in poverty, there is a general distrust of anyone in a position of authority. This means you will often be immediately mistrusted by parents. There are many different reasons parents from poverty may not come to parent-teacher conferences: They are working two jobs, they do not

have transportation, they do not have childcare, they are English language learners and do not understand you well enough, or maybe they speak only casual register and the formal-register words that are used in school make them uncomfortable or do not make sense, etc.

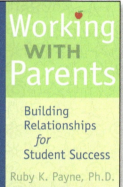

Furthermore, when parents from poverty come to the school, they are often angry. Parents from poverty will come up to school when they believe there is a disrespect issue. To have better strategies for dealing with parents, please see my book *Working with Parents.*

This flyer communicates the bare essentials with simple language and inviting images.

It is important to make it clear that food and childcare will be provided.

These are real incentives when you are asking people, many of them single parents, to come up to the school right at dinnertime.

EXAMPLE

Communicating with parents in poverty can be difficult. Poverty often limits people's need for formal-register language, so parents may not know the terminology of school, and this can be frustrating and confusing for everyone. Make your communication with all parents simpler, quicker to read, and easier to understand.

> **M**ake your communication with all parents simpler, quicker to read, and easier to understand.

Parents from poverty will be more comfortable, and middle class and wealthy parents will appreciate the efficiency as well.

What?
A meeting for parents

Where?
The school

What time?
7:00 p.m.

Food?
Yes

Childcare?
Yes

The following overview of two different parenting styles is based on information from the book *Unequal Childhoods* by Annette Lareau

	Concerted cultivation	Accomplishment of natural growth
Key elements	Parent actively fosters and assesses child's talents, opinions, and skills	Parent cares for child and allows child to grow
Organization of daily life	Multiple child leisure activities orchestrated by adults	"Hanging out," particularly with kin, by child
Language use	Reasoning, directives Child contestation of adult statements Extended negotiations between parents and child	Directives Rare questioning or challenging of adults by child General acceptance by child of directives
Interventions in institutions	Criticisms and interventions on behalf of the child Training of child to take on this role	Dependence on institutions Sense of powerlessness and frustration Conflict between child-rearing practices at home and school
Consequences	Emerging sense of entitlement on the part of the child	Emerging sense of constraint on the part of the child

Lareau studied both black and white families at both the poverty and middle-class levels of economics. What the study found is that the differentiating factor in discipline was not race but economic level. Both black and white families in the middle class taught their children to negotiate institutions, while both black and white families from poverty taught their children to react strongly to or avoid institutions.

How Do Parents Tend to Parent in Poverty?

In "Targeting Parenting in Early Childhood: A Public Health Approach to Improve Outcomes for Children Living in Poverty," Morris et al. look at families in poverty and how parenting behaviors impact children. The study used parent self-reporting and observational assessments. Single-parent families with a father do better than single-parent families with a mother. Maternal depressive symptoms may be a part of the difference.

A study from Krueger et al. found that married-couple households, regardless of socioeconomic factors, fare better than other models in shielding children from adverse factors such as lack of healthcare or lower cognitive outcomes.

Krueger et al. conclude: "U.S. children increasingly live in family structures that are associated with poor child well-being. The links between childhood circumstances and socio-economic and health outcomes in later life mean that children's disadvantages may persist throughout their lives."

Lareau finds that middle-class parents practice a kind of parenting she calls "concerted cultivation."

Working-class and poor parents promote what she calls "the accomplishment of natural growth."

Both parenting styles are motivated by the parents' love for the children.

17 Will the Principal Support Me?

tldr: The level of support the principal provides is important. There are many ways to gauge that level of support, including looking at campus planning, student selection, even how clean the bathrooms are. Support ≠ popularity; a successful principal will not be well-loved by all. What are reasonable and unreasonable expectations for support from the principal? If you do not have a supportive principal, work closely with other teachers, post an introductory video of yourself for parents, and set up classroom management systems.

One of the most critical aspects of your first years of teaching is the level of support you receive from your principal. How do you know that you will be working for a principal who will support you? Provide good guidance and advice? If you have an out-of-control student, what kinds of support are available to you?

Ask Ruby: What Do You Do When You Cannot Get Administrative Support?

Full resources/videos available at *ahaprocess.com/byqt*

Does the principal attend difficult parent meetings with you to provide a buffer, or are you on your own?

How do you find out? There are several ways to do that. One is to look at the building. Is it clean? Go into the student bathrooms. Are they clean? When a principal is paying attention to the well-being of students, buildings and bathrooms are clean. How are you greeted when you arrive? Are they glad to see you? Do they ignore you? That is how you will be treated when you are a teacher there.

Ask these questions: How much collegial planning and work is done on the campus? What is the achievement level on the campus? How long has it been that way? If the principal has been there for more than three years and the achievement has not climbed, there is a leadership problem. See the subsequent rubrics on the qualities of expert principals for more.

How are students selected for classrooms? Does the principal select them, or does the principal let the teachers decide who gets which students?

If there is a weak principal, existing teachers will sometimes give the most difficult students to the new teachers.

Does the principal attend difficult parent meetings with you to provide a buffer, or are you on your own?

Does the principal have the strength to stand up to faculty bullies and difficult, unreasonable parents? Does the principal insist on ethical behavior for self and others? Does the principal keep promises? Does the principal talk about faculty members behind their backs? Does the principal have favorite staff members?

How much time does the principal spend in the building? If the principal is always gone, the campus tends to suffer. What kind of central office support does the principal have? If the principal has no support in the central office, then it is difficult for the principal to support you.

> **N**ot everyone will like a successful principal, but respect is key.

A couple points to remember: Not everyone will like a successful principal, but respect is key. Principals have to tell people no, and they have to insist on standards of behavior and performance. Not everyone is going to like that. Obviously, if no one has anything good to say about the principal, that is a sign that something is wrong. But it is also true that if no one has anything BAD to say about a principal, that is not good either. The key thing to listen for is respect. Does the principal have respect? Are the principal's decisions respected even when the decisions are not liked?

What are reasonable expectations of supports from a principal?

1. They will not allow you to continue in an unsafe condition or with a dangerous student—one who will seriously harm you. They will seek alternative placement for that student.

2. They will provide teaching and learning opportunities for you—including a supportive staff member (mentor) who will help you, answer questions, etc.

3. They will intervene when a parent is difficult, harassing, or inappropriate.

4. They will provide interventions and periodic relief when a student repeatedly has difficulties outside the norm.

5. The campus itself will be safe and clean.

6. They will protect you from faculty members who are bullies.

What are **unreasonable** expectations of support from a principal?

1. It is unreasonable to expect that the principal will fix every issue in your classroom. Part of your responsibility is to know your students and establish relationships of mutual respect. For example, if you have a homeless student, you should know that the student is homeless, and you should know that the student may not be able to keep track of materials, homework, etc.

2. It is unreasonable to expect that you can send every difficult student to the principal every day. Principals have 25–50 teachers on a campus. It is simply not possible for them to handle every difficult student's issues every day.

3. It is unreasonable to expect that the principal will continually make exceptions for you if you are late, do not meet deadlines, fail to do the necessary paperwork, etc. To be treated with respect in your job, you must treat your job with respect.

What do you do when you do not have a supportive principal?

1. Find out who the best teachers are on campus, and ask them how they handle certain problems and issues. Use their suggestions. Develop relationships with them.

2. Do contacts/visits of your students' homes with another teacher. Establish as many good relationships with parents as you can. It will make your life so much easier. If you do not make home visits/contacts, call each parent each semester/year before school starts, and tell them you are glad to be their child's teacher. That way if you have to contact them because there is a problem, they have heard a positive message from you first.

3. Make a video of yourself on your phone. Ask your principal if you can put it on the school website and social media accounts. Share the video with parents.

   DO NOT MAKE THE VIDEO LONGER THAN TWO MINUTES.

   In the video, introduce yourself, show the classroom, and give viewers a way to contact you if they need to do so.

4. Set up good classroom management systems and positive behavior systems.

18 What Do You Do When You Have a Difficult Principal? What Is a Difficult Principal?

tldr: A difficult principal actively makes your job more difficult. Harassment, unreasonable demands, and lies are just a few markers of difficult principals. If you work for one, find a new job if you can. Study the school board in the district you want to work in. If you can't move to a new job, learn to "manage up" by asking which of your efforts will be supported and which efforts will not.

Full resources/videos available at ahaprocess.com/byqt

There are many variations on the theme of "difficult principal," and these are some of them:

❏ Unreasonably demanding

❏ Requires lesson plans that take 2–3 hours to do daily

❏ Insists on reams of unnecessary paperwork

❏ Requires that you put in long hours every week for extra meetings, training, etc.

❏ Verbally berates you in front of staff, parents, and/or students

❏ Tells you one thing and does another

❏ Sexually or verbally harasses you

❏ Allows you to be harassed by staff members and does not intervene to stop it

❏ Monitors things that are not important

❏ Wastes staff meeting time

❏ Frequently interrupts over the PA system

❏ Constantly changes the direction of initiatives

❏ Is usually unavailable

❏ Is not aware of what is going on in the building

What should you do if you have a difficult principal?

MY RECOMMENDATION IS TO FIND ANOTHER TEACHING POSITION!

But BEFORE YOU DO THAT, do this homework:

Look at the school district you want to work in. Read their board agendas, minutes, and briefs, which are public documents.

What you are looking for is the following information:

1. How often does the board have meetings?
2. How long are the meetings?
3. How many split votes does the board have? (Example: A five-member board has a lot of 3–2 votes.)
4. How much time does the board spend in executive session?

The longer and more frequent the board meetings, the more split votes, and the more executive sessions, the greater the odds are that the school board is fighting and unstable. You do not want a job in that district because the principal has difficulty getting board and district support. When a principal cannot get support, it becomes very difficult for the principal to support the staff.

Full resources/videos available at ahaprocess.com/byqt

If the school board is fairly stable and effective, then you want to inquire about particular principals. Ask a parent who has a student in that building about the principal. Ask a couple of teachers about their principal.

Maybe you have a difficult principal but you can't leave your job, maybe you don't want to leave, or maybe you do leave and you wind up with another difficult principal anyway. Well, what can you do to get extra support from the principal? In other words, how do you "manage up?"

1. Be on time.
2. Get your paperwork done on time.
3. Save your arguments for things that matter. Do not argue simply because you don't "like" something.
4. Don't be a gossip or a lounge lizard, and don't create a lot of faculty dissension or stir up trouble.
5. Be respectful of the principal's time. An average principal has 40+ staff. They cannot give all of their time to you.
6. Forewarn your principal of issues that may come to them. Administrators do not like surprises. If you have an angry parent, make sure the principal knows. If you have a discipline issue that you think will end up in the principal's office, give the principal as much advance warning as possible.

Before You Quit Teaching • 18: Difficult Principal

When I was a principal, I would go to my assistant superintendent and say, "I have these issues I would like to address in my building next year. I know every one of these issues may become a school board issue. I also know that you supervise 18 principals, and you cannot take the heat on every issue for all 18 of us. So which of these issues can I work on next year with your support?"

> **So which of these areas can I focus on and count on you to support me?**

If you follow these practices, especially the simple ones like being on time and doing your paperwork, you can make an impression on even the most difficult of principals. You can also adapt my model with my assistant superintendent to your relationship with your principal. Warn the principal of issues that may come their way, but also be aware that they can't help every teacher with every issue. Say to your principal, "In the next year, I have these four areas I'd like to work on. I know you have 50 teachers in this building, and you can't support every single one of them in every single area.

"So which of these areas can I focus on and count on you to support me?" Many difficult principals will see that you are trying to help them limit their workload. The hope is that a small gesture like this will get you more support—or at least more leeway—in the future.

19 Colleagues—Will They Help Me or Hinder Me?

tldr: Both! Colleagues can hurt you and help you. There is a pecking order among teachers. Find the power brokers. Survival is easier in high-poverty schools when teachers have each other's backs. Every campus has a diverse cast of characters. Ally yourself with teachers who are respected, and be sure to make friends with the custodian and the school secretary.

Colleagues can be the greatest gifts of your teaching career and of your life. They can also be the most exasperating facets of your work and life as well. They become a family of sorts—you often spend more time interacting with them than with your own family. And as we know, families can have both functional and dysfunctional aspects. Your "work family" is no different.

First of all, you should know that there is a power structure among the teachers. Because teachers have tenure, many of them have stayed at the same campus for years. Not only do they know the history of the campus, the district, and the community, they know two or three generations of families, board members, other administrators, and influential community members. And so even though they are all "teachers," some have significantly more political clout than others.

Full resources/videos available at ahaprocess.com/byqt

How do you figure out quickly who the power brokers among the teachers are?

Find out the following:

How long have they been teaching in the district?

Who do they know on the board?

Whose political campaign(s) have they been involved with?

Who do they socialize with?

Are they a member of the country club? Etc.

Basically, find out who is politically involved and/or has a long history with the district. These are the people who tend to have more relationship power in school and district politics.

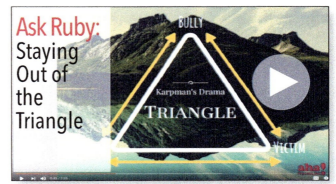

Secondly, in for-profit business, there is a financial bottom line, but in the school business, the bottom line is survival.

Because high-poverty schools always have insufficient resources, it becomes imperative that teachers work together so that survival occurs. There is a clear understanding in high-poverty schools that you have to "watch each other's backs" because you don't know when a student might have a crisis, when resources will be cut again, when the district will change directions, or when the laws that mandate what you have to do will change.

When I was a principal, on my staff I had the following: several extraordinary teachers, two faculty bullies, a teacher who was also a union rep, a librarian who hated kids, two teachers with serious mental health issues, a beginning teacher who was extraordinary, a beginning teacher who was struggling with discipline, a beginning teacher who was struggling to get academic performance, and two teachers who were close to retirement and simply coasting. Most campuses are no different.

AHA! PROCESS PRESENTS

Virtual Coaching

Virtual coaching uses video, phone, and email to bring expert consultants to you for tailored and trusted strategies, feedback, debriefing, and consulting.

110 Full resources/videos available at *ahaprocess.com/byqt*

How Do You Know Who to Form Alliances With?

1. **Watch closely in faculty meetings: Which teachers do the other teachers respect?**
   (Not fear, but respect.) One indicator of a very good teacher is that parents, students, and other teachers respect them.

2. **Of those teachers who have respect, are any of them in your grade level or course area?**
   Have they taught your grade level or course area?
   Would you respect what they have to tell you?

3. **Instruction can come as much from the teachers you want to be like as from the teachers you do not want to be like.**
   Everyone has something you can learn from. Refer to the rubrics for skilled teachers to find behaviors to watch for and emulate.

4. **Make sure you have a good relationship with the following people:** the counselor, the custodian, and the school secretary (the custodian and secretary tend to know everything that is going on in the building—VERY IMPORTANT), the psychologist, the nurse, the media specialist, any teacher assistants, and the principal and assistant principal. And, if possible, try also to get to know one person in the central office.

Colleagues can pose challenges, but they can also bring great satisfaction and joy to your job. If you have each other's backs, you can all do more with the time you are able to devote to curriculum and instruction.

20 Curriculum and Instruction—
I Only Have So Much Time...

tldr: You will never have enough (instructional) time, but you can make the most of the time you have. Look at the big picture: state test scores + standards + district guide + school calendar = everything you need to manage time effectively. Find good teachers and ask to see examples of student work. Testing is frustrating, and so is the testing schedule, but don't panic. Instead, be prepared.

That is the problem in a nutshell: TIME. You can teach almost anything if you have enough time. And the problem of lack of time is exacerbated when you teach students from poverty because they usually come into school lagging a little behind their peers who come from middle-class households. And you are supposed to catch them up in one year.

Ruby Payne
Curriculum and Instruction

To have high achievement, if you are in a subject or grade level that is tested, it is important to consider your students' test scores on the state assessment from the previous year, your state standards, your district teaching guide, and the calendar for the school year.

112   Full resources/videos available at *ahaprocess.com/byqt*

> One of the most important concepts to bring with you into teaching is PAYOFF FOR TIME.

In other words, you want to look at what your students know (test scores), what is supposed to be taught this year (standards), what the district has indicated should be taught (district guides), and how much time you have to teach it (calendar). If you are going to be successful, you have to plot your teaching against TIME. Because you are tested against time.

One of the most important concepts to bring with you into teaching is PAYOFF FOR TIME. In other words, for the amount of time you spent on it, did you get a payoff? That is, did you see high achievement scores? You will want to get the book *Research-Based Strategies*. For every strategy, the effect size tells you what the payoff in achievement is. For example, if you make students plan their grade, you will see almost three years of growth in one year.

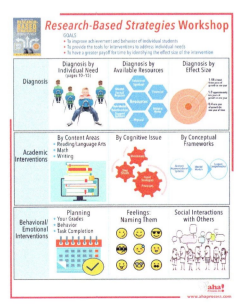

Research-Based Strategies Workshop at a Glance

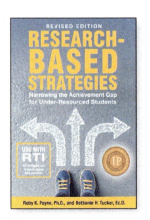

Easily find the interventions you need in the menu-driven *Research-Based Strategies.*

The research is that good teachers know where the majority of students will be performing at the end of the year. Find some good teachers in your subject area or grade level, and ask them to show you examples of the kind of work they want their students to be doing at the end of the year. That will give you an idea of where you want your students to be.

Reality of Testing

One of the issues that will cause you frustration is the incredible amount of testing you will be required to do with students. One of the things that will help you deal with this is having the testing AND testing preparation schedules before the year begins.

FREE webinar:
Developing Student Expertise

Find out how much formative testing is required.

Is it weekly?
Once every grading period?
How much time does it take?
Who scores it?
Will you get to see the results?

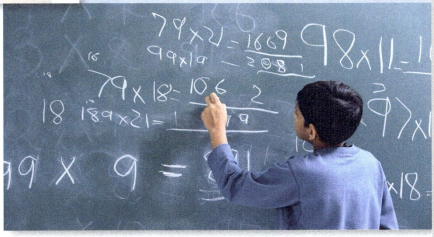

Make Sure You Understand the Testing Schedule Before the School Year Starts

The testing schedule is often so unreasonable that it seems ridiculous. But it will play a key role in your evaluation. Don't panic! Just make sure you understand it.

V Realities of Teaching

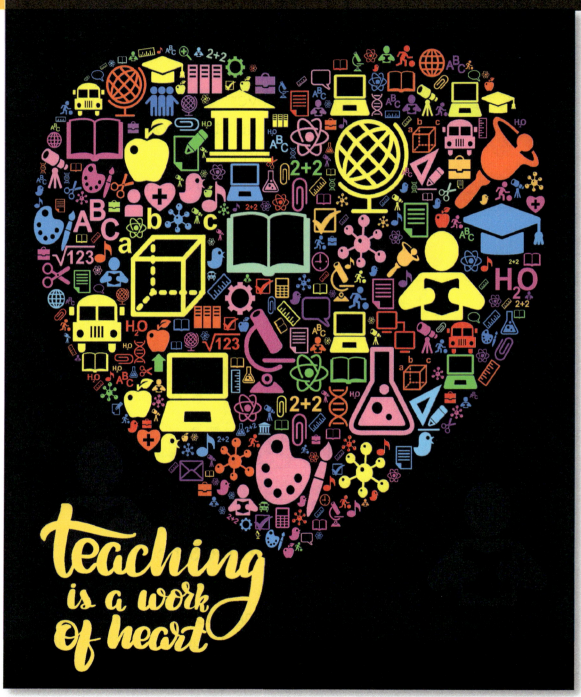

21 Issues at the Middle and Secondary Levels

tldr: Do make friends with department chairs. Don't get too friendly with students. Guard personal information carefully. Go to the principal with any and all legal and ethical questions.

If you are a beginning teacher at the secondary level, here are some dos and don'ts:

1. **Find out who your department chair is, and make friends.** If you make friends with the department chair, you are less likely to get stuck with five preparations your first and second year.

2. **If they ask you to teach a class out of your content area, make friends with that department chair also.** Ask if you can have the lesson plans from another teacher who is certified in that content and teaches that course.

3. **Remember that you are very close in age to your students. DO NOT GET CONFUSED AND THINK OF THEM AS FRIENDS.** There are ethical and legal lines that cannot be crossed. Here are some guidelines that will help you:

   a. Do not go to parties that high school students have—even if you are invited.

   b. Do not be in a room with the door closed with any one student alone—and it does not matter what gender the student is.

   c. Do not talk about a student in front of other students. Even praise can sometimes be misconstrued as gossip.

   d. Do not disclose personal information about any student to any other student.

   e. Do not disclose personal information about a student to a "friend" of the parent.

   f. If you have any questions about the ethics or legality of a situation, ask your principal.

22 Working Conditions

Ruby Payne
Should I Take a Job in This School District?

tldr: Facilities in high-poverty schools may be inadequate. Tour the campus before you take the job, and be sure to check the student bathrooms. Know that you can't change a whole campus and culture on your own.

Many schools with a large population of students in poverty have poor working conditions.

The rooms are old, often with inadequate heating or cooling. The bathrooms are ancient. A/V and other technology often does not work. The district may not have sufficient Internet bandwidth. The list can go on and on.

Before you take the job, ask for a tour of the campus. Ask to see the room you will be in, the library, the gym, and the teachers' workroom.

Most important? BE SURE TO SEE THE STUDENT BATHROOMS. The condition of the student bathrooms will tell you a great deal about the working conditions. Based upon what you see, you will need to decide if you can work in those conditions.

Some new teachers approach a school with inadequate conditions as though it is their mission to make the whole school better. This is noble, but it is also these teachers who burn out the soonest. Each school has its own reality, and as an individual teacher, it is difficult to change that reality.

23 Politics, Morale, and Unions

tldr: When teacher and student absenteeism are high, morale is bad. Schools are political systems. The advantages of joining the union are greater in some states than in others.

Every school district I have ever been involved in has told me that morale is BAD and is only getting worse.

If someone doesn't like an administrator, this is the insult hurled at them most often, that morale in the school is way down and declining steadily. The real proof of morale is in absenteeism, both teacher absenteeism and student absenteeism. When absenteeism is high, then yes—morale is bad. But if teacher and student attendance are good, other things in the school will be working smoothly as well.

There will always be politics in education. In fact, schools are really just political systems whose by product is education. But they are first and foremost a political system. Schools have boards that are elected or appointed, and they are subject to the laws passed by the legislature.

At least some of their funding comes from the government—even in most private schools. I can't say it loudly enough: SCHOOLS ARE POLITICAL SYSTEMS. I often hear the lament that schools should not be political. They are political, and as a new teacher I want you to be prepared for that and to know how to succeed.

Teachers unions—do you join or not?
Depends on your state laws—whether your state is a right-to-work state or not. As a beginning teacher, union leadership knows that in most states you do not have tenure for the first 2–3 years. They also know that the newest staff members are the first to get cut if there is a reduction in employees. Unions typically work to protect the rights of tenured members, although that is not always the case.

To better understand the thinking of unions, read the book *Rules for Radicals* by Saul Alinsky.

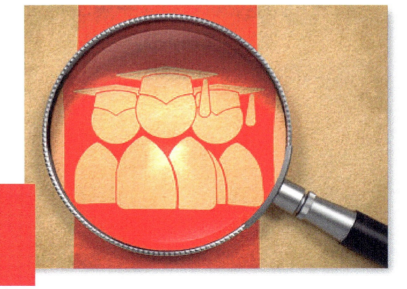

Schools are political systems

24 Emotional Realities of Teaching: How to Handle the Grieving

tldr: Standing with students who are in emotional need is the hardest and most rewarding part of the job. There are strategies you can use to put the emotional issues in perspective.

The hardest parts of teaching for me are the emotional events and involvements that occur.

Let me tell you a story.

When I was a principal, my secretary once interrupted a meeting I was in and said, "I need you to come out of the meeting."

I followed her out of the room, and there was a man standing there in the hall who said to me, "I have a kid from this school with me, a sixth-grader. His father was killed last night in a car accident about 2 a.m. I am his neighbor. The kid insisted he wanted to come to school today. I told his mother I would bring him, but now he will not get out of the car. I have to go to work. I don't understand why he had to come to school."

I said to the neighbor, "He came to school today because it is one of the few places in his life that is the same. He knows his life is forever different now, and so he's seeking the safety of routine."

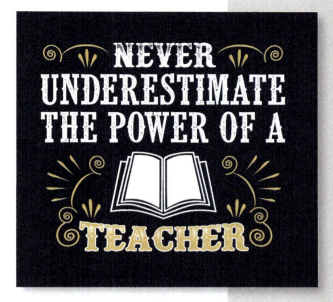

I went out to the car, got the student, and brought him into my office. I told him that if at any time he needed to leave and go home, he could come to the office and I would arrange it. I told him he could not leave without telling me, but if he came to me first, I would excuse him. I will never forget his face or the grief his neighbor clearly shared.

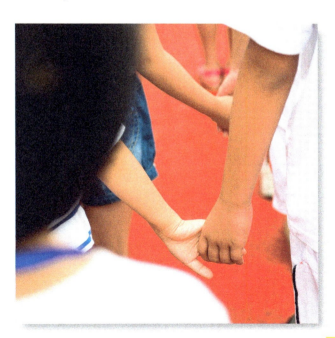

FREE webinar:
Address emotional poverty and build emotional wealth in your students

How do you put the emotional issues in perspective?

1. **RECOGNIZE THE LEGAL ISSUES.**
   Make sure you follow the legal requirements of your state that cover the reporting of abuse.

2. **UNDERSTAND THE IMPACT ON STUDENTS.**
   Emotional Poverty has a lot of information about how emotional issues can arise from situations that make you feel less than and separate from.

3. **DO NOT PITY.**
   Pity is a form of abuse and clearly communicates that the individual is not capable of dealing with the situation.

4. **RESPECT THE STRENGTH OF THE INDIVIDUAL.**
   Say to the student: "I respect your incredible strength in this situation. How can I support you?"

5. **KNOW YOUR LIMITS.**
   Be very clear with yourself: You are not God. You cannot fix everything.

6. **SHOW EMPATHY AND KINDNESS.**
   Empathy and kindness are the fastest ways to establish your authenticity and build trust with students.

7. **MAKE FRIENDS WITH THE SCHOOL COUNSELOR.**
   Talk to the school counselor yourself. Refer students to the counselor if you think it will help them.

8. **REMEMBER THE GIFTS YOU CAN GIVE STUDENTS:**
   A future story, daily kindness, a smile, skill development, an education.

25 Conclusion

Teaching is a calling. If you come into teaching with hope, resources, and a future story, you will be able to gift those same things on to the next generation. The rewards you will reap are so amazing. Your students will remember you long after you're gone, and that is deeper and more meaningful than monetary rewards will ever be.

Ruby Payne Wraps Up *Before You Quit Teaching*

 Complete our survey and get a $15 coupon to use in our webstore.
Excludes shipping.
ahaprocess.com/byqt-survey

Expert Secondary Principal Rubric

	BEGINNING	DEVELOPING	CAPABLE	EXPERT
Safe and culturally competent learning environment	Arbitrary discipline. Little analysis by race or class or gender of building patterns. Unsafe physical and verbal environment.	Discipline tends to be punitive rather than instructive. Focus is on individual student rather than overall structures, patterns, approaches. Individuals are not confronted (80% of referrals come from 11% of staff and 90% of referrals come from 10% of students). Staff bullies students.	Structures safe environment and monitors safety—verbally, physically, emotionally. Cultural competencies are evident. Students and staff feel safe. Discipline interactions are designed to be instructive and supportive rather than punitive.	Extremely safe and calm environment. Inclusive and relational by intent and design. Sexism, racism, bullying, etc. are not tolerated. Students are involved in creating safety. Multiple monitors are developed to enhance well-being.
Operations (budgets, buildings, staff, central office relationships)	Facility poorly maintained and not repaired. Dirty. Budget is messy. Not exactly sure of how many staff or students. Few procedures for anything. Badmouths and blames central office.	Building somewhat clean. Budget mistakes but uses budget according to guidelines. Tolerates central office. Tardy with written reports. Follows district procedures and policies most of time.	Follows and uses budget for student well-being. Reports are on time. Relationships with central office are congenial. Building is clean. Repairs are made. Follows district policies.	Skilled and innovative with budget to meet student/staff needs. Building well-kept. Staff organization is excellent, procedures are outlined, roles are defined, communication is smooth and timely. Develops relationships with central office to enhance campus operations.
Student achievement	Pays little attention to it. Focuses on daily crises. Does not participate in developing schedule. Few positive interactions with students. Blames students or parents.	Interacts with students. Knows problem students and "heroes." Little understanding of student achievement. Makes arbitrary decisions during teacher evaluation about students. Very little understanding of learning.	Knows half of students by name. Is in the halls. Talks to students. Asks about their courses. Has data on course and class achievement. Meets with departments to identify ways to provide support for greater student achievement.	Clarifies and maintains role of protector of high student performance. Structures schedule, department performance, and counselors to enhance student achievement. Keenly aware of student data.

Expert Secondary Principal Rubric

	BEGINNING	DEVELOPING	CAPABLE	EXPERT
Staff performance	Few expectations for staff. Faculty bullies run building. Wants loyalty rather than performance. Little interest in instruction.	Knows most staff by name. Staff meetings focus on students and instruction—not operations. Can confront individual staff members. Uses walk-throughs to monitor staff.	Focuses staff performance using data and student work. Structures PLC (professional learning community) to focus on student performance. Monitors department performance as it relates to student achievement. Seeks professional development for staff.	Holds staff to high expectations. Provides the support so those can be reached. Teacher expertise developed. No tolerance for underperformance of staff. Provides excellent staff development.
Community/ parent outreach and communication	Parents are not welcome. Website and social media are limited. Does not have a positive image in the community.	Bad public relations. Limited communication and involvement with parents and community. Sees the campus as separate from the community.	Sees the campus as an integral part of the community. Regularly seeks opinion outside of campus. Uses multiple communication mechanisms. Does not necessarily seek positive public relations.	Builds a deep network of relationships outside of campus. Structures and encourages parent involvement via video, website, social media, email, paper handouts and flyers, etc. Sees parents as vital to school community. Seeks positive public relations for building.

	BEGINNING	DEVELOPING	CAPABLE	EXPERT
Conflict resolution and management skills	Needs to be liked. Poor or no decisions. Blames others. Promises mean little. May exacerbate conflict.	Procrastinates or uses win/lose approach. Unpredictable responses. Gathers only part of the data. Has difficulty separating the person from the issue.	Uses a win/win approach. Does not participate in triangulation. Keeps promises. Needs to be respected. Focuses on the issue rather than the person.	Identifies boundaries of decision: BATNA (Best Alternative To a Negotiated Agreement). Has high integrity. Makes decisions against well-being of students. Builds climate of participation and mutual respect.
Student, sports, and extracurricular activities	Focuses on favorite sport or activity. Little attention to the big picture or participation.	Tries to be unbiased in support. Does not focus much on equitable participation by gender, race, or talent.	Overtly seeks participation and involvement. Knows results of activities. Attends when possible. Emphasizes academics, as well as sports.	Focuses on win/win. Makes certain almost every student participates. Makes certain that all activities are sponsored and supported. Involves students in development.

Before You Quit Teaching • **Bonus: Expert Secondary Principal Rubric**

Expert Elementary Principal Rubric

	BEGINNING	DEVELOPING	CAPABLE	EXPERT
Safe and culturally competent learning environment	Arbitrary discipline. Little analysis of building patterns by race or class or gender. Unsafe physical and verbal environment.	Discipline tends to be punitive rather than instructive. Focus is on individual student rather than overall structures, patterns, approaches. Individuals are not confronted (80% of referrals come from 11% of staff and 90% of referrals come from 10% of students). Staff bullies students.	Structures a safe environment and monitors the safety—verbally, physically, emotionally. Cultural competencies are evident. Students and staff feel safe. Discipline interactions are designed to be instructive, supportive, rather than punitive.	Extremely safe and calm environment. Inclusive and relational by intent and design. Sexism, racism, bullying, etc. are not tolerated. Students are involved in creating the safety. Multiple monitors are developed to enhance well-being.
Operations (budgets, buildings, staff, central office relationships)	Facility poorly maintained and repaired. Dirty. Budget is messy. Not exactly sure of how many staff or students. Few procedures for anything. Badmouths and blames central office.	Building somewhat clean. Budget mistakes but uses budget according to guidelines. Tolerates central office. Tardy with written reports. Follows district procedures and policies most of the time.	Follows and uses the budget for student well-being. Reports are on time. Relationships with central office are congenial. Building is clean. Repairs are made. Follows district policies.	Skilled and innovative with the budget to meet student/staff needs. Building well-kept. Staff organization is excellent, procedures outlined, roles defined, communication smooth and timely. Develops relationships with central office to enhance campus operations.
Student achievement	Pays little attention to it. Focuses on daily crises. Does not participate in developing schedule. Few positive interactions with students. Blames students or parents.	Interacts with students. Knows the problem students and the "heroes." Little understanding of student achievement. Makes arbitrary decisions about students during teacher evaluation. Very little understanding of learning.	Knows half of students by name. Is in the halls. Talks to students. Asks about their courses. Has data on course and class achievement. Meets with departments to identify ways to provide support for greater student achievement.	Clarifies and maintains role of protector of high student performance. Structures schedule, department performance, and counselors to enhance student achievement. Keenly aware of student data.

	BEGINNING	DEVELOPING	CAPABLE	EXPERT
Staff performance	Few expectations for staff. Faculty bullies run building. Wants loyalty rather than performance. Little interest in instruction.	Knows most staff by name. Staff meetings focus on students and instruction not operations. Can confront individual staff members. Uses walk-throughs to monitor staff.	Focuses staff performance using data and student work. Structures PLC (professional learning community) to focus on student performance. Monitors department performance as it relates to student achievement. Seeks professional development for staff.	Holds staff to high expectations. Provides the support so those can be reached. Teacher expertise developed. No tolerance for underperformance of staff. Provides excellent staff development.
Community/ parent outreach and communication	Parents are not welcome. Website is limited. Does not have a positive image in the community.	Bad public relations. Limited communication and involvement with parents and community. Sees the campus as separate from the community.	Sees the campus as an integral part of the community. Regularly seeks opinions outside of campus. Uses multiple communication mechanisms. Does not necessarily seek positive public relations.	Builds a deep network of relationships outside of campus. Structures and encourages parent involvement via video, website, social media, email, paper, etc. Sees parents as vital to school community. Seeks positive public relations for the building.
Conflict resolution and management skills	Needs to be liked. Makes poor decisions or no decisions at all. Blames others. Promises mean little because they aren't kept. May exacerbate conflicts.	Procrastinates or uses win/lose approach. Unpredictable responses. Gathers only part of the data. Has difficulty separating the person from the issue.	Uses a win/win approach. Does not participate in triangulation. Keeps promises. Needs to be respected. Focuses on the issue rather than the person.	Identifies the boundaries of the decision: BATNA (Best Alternative To a Negotiated Agreement). Has high integrity. Makes decisions against well-being of students. Builds a climate of participation and mutual respect. Focuses on win/win.
Reading instruction	Sticks with a program with no variation. Does not know what an expert reader is. Few diagnostic tools provided. Relies on individual teacher reporting and test scores. Heavy emphasis on worksheets. Grouping is rigid.	Allows some variation in the program. Mostly concerned about the lowest readers. Little attention to top third of readers. Reading instruction is mostly confined to reading time. Little time given to actual reading. Grouping is occasionally redone.	Has a diagnostic approach to each student as reader regardless of program used. Reading instruction is integrated across content. Monitors test scores and actual performance as a reader. Uses multiple formats for reading.	Uses a growth model for students as readers that each student helps plan against five characteristics of a skilled reader (strategic, fluent, motivated, comprehension, and uses a process). Involves parents in the growth plan.

Selected Bibliography

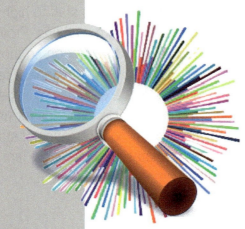

Alinsky, S. (1971). *Rules for radicals: A pragmatic primer for realistic radicals.* New York, NY: Random House.

Callahan, R., with Trubo, R. (2002). *Tapping the healer within: Using thought-field therapy to instantly conquer your fears, anxieties, and emotional distress*. New York, NY: McGraw-Hill Education.

Clifton, J. (2016, May 11). Millennials: How they live and work. Gallup. Retrieved from https://news.gallup.com/opinion/chairman/ 191426/millennials-live-work.aspx

Covey, S. (1989). *The 7 habits of highly effective people.* New York, NY: Free Press.

Deaton, A. (2018, Jan. 24). The U.S. can no longer hide from its deep poverty problem. *The New York Times.* Retrieved from https://www.nytimes.com/2018/01/24/opinion/poverty-united-states.html

Dias-Lacy, S. L., & Guirguis, R. V. (2017). Challenges for new teachers and ways of coping with them. *Journal of Education and Learning, 6*(3), 265–272. doi:10.5539/jel.v6n3p265

Field, G. (1986). The psychological deficits and treatment needs of chronic criminality. *Federal Probation, 50*(4), 60–66. Retrieved from https://psycnet.apa.org/record/1988-10918-001

Jay, M. (2013). *The defining decade: Why your twenties matter.* New York, NY: Hachette.

Karpman, S. (1968). Fairy tales and script drama analysis. *Transactional Analysis Bulletin, 7*(26), 39–43.

Krueger, P. M., Jutte, D. P., Franzini, L., Elo, I., & Hayward, M. D. (2015). *Population Health Metrics, 13*(6). doi:10.1186/s12963-015-0038-0

Full resources/videos available at *ahaprocess.com/byqt*

Lareau, A. (2003). *Unequal childhoods: Class, race and family life.* Berkeley, CA: University of California Press.

Mind Movies. (2019). Homepage. Retrieved from https://www.mindmovies.com

Morris, A. S., Robinson, L. R., Hays-Grudo, J., Claussen, A. H., Hartwig, S. A., & Treat, A. E. (2017). *Child Development, 88*(2), 388–397. doi:10.1111/cdev.12743

Payne, R. K. (2006). *Working with parents—building relationships for student success.* Highlands, TX: aha! Process.

Payne, R. K. (2006). *Working with students: Discipline strategies for the classroom.* Highlands, TX: aha! Process.

Payne, R. K., & Tucker, B. H. (2017). *Research-based strategies: Narrowing the achievement gap for under-resourced students* (rev. ed.). Highlands, TX: aha! Process.

Payne, R. K. (2018). *Emotional poverty in all demographics: How to reduce anger, anxiety, and violence in the classroom.* Highlands, TX: aha! Process.

Payne, R. K. (2019). *A framework for understanding poverty: A cognitive approach* (6th rev. ed.). Highlands, TX: aha! Process.

Procedures check for secondary teachers. (n.d.). Retrieved from https://www.stcloudstate.edu/ignite/_files/documents/classroom-management/procedures-secondary.pdf

Schleckser, J. (2017, November 21). If you work with your mind, there's no retirement for you. *Inc.* Retrieved from https://www.inc.com/jim-schleckser/there-is-no-retirement-and-thats-a-good-thing.html

Sheehy, G. (2006). *Passages: Predictable crises of adult life* (30th anniversary ed.). New York, NY: Ballantine.

Walker, R. J. (2008). Twelve characteristics of an effective teacher: A longitudinal, qualitative, quasi-research study of in-service and pre-service teachers' opinions. *Educational Horizons, 87*(1), 61–68. Retrieved from https://files.eric.ed.gov/fulltext/EJ815372.pdf

Additional Resources

Read *Before You Quit Teaching* online for free!
ahaprocess.com/byqt

Join us on Facebook
facebook.com/rubypayne
facebook.com/bridgesoutofpoverty
facebook.com/workplacestability
facebook.com/ahaprocess
facebook.com/collegeachievementalliance

Twitter
@ahaprocess
#povertychat
#BridgesOutofPoverty

Subscribe to our YouTube channel
youtube.com/ahaprocess

Read our blog
www.ahaprocess.com/blog

Instagram
@ahaprocess

Free webinar series
https://www.ahaprocess.com/free-webinar-series/